Index Kitchen Library

One-pot

Creamy Tomato and Chicken Stew, page 37

Moroccan Lamb Shaks, page 17

Cioppino, page 89

All recipes are double-tested by our team of home economists. When we test our recipes, we rate them for ease of preparation. The following cookery ratings are on the recipes in this book, making them easy to use and understand.

A single Cooking with Confidence symbol indicates a recipe that is simple and generally quick to make—perfect for beginners.

Two symbols indicate the need for just a little more care and a little more time.

Three symbols indicate special dishes that need more investment in time, care and patience—but the results are worth it.

The Publisher thanks the following for their assistance: Chief Australia, Sunbeam Corporation, Kambrook, Sheldon & Hammond, Southcorp Appliances, Bertoli Olive Oil, Dinosaur Designs, Style Lamination and The Bay Tree.

IMPORTANT

Those who might be at risk from the effects of salmonella food poisoning (the elderly, pregnant women, young children and those suffering from immune deficiency diseases) should consult their GP with any concerns about eating raw eggs.

CONTENTS

Channa Masala, page 106

Spicy Beef, Potato and Capsicum Stew, page 21

NAVARIN OF LAMB

Preparation time: 25 minutes
Total cooking time: 1 hour 35 minutes
Serves 4

8 lamb noisettes
plain flour, seasoned with salt
   and pepper
2 tablespoons oil
2 sticks celery, sliced diagonally
   into 2 cm (¾ inch) lengths
12 baby carrots, peeled
12 new potatoes, unpeeled
6 sprigs of thyme
¼ cup (15 g/½ oz) chopped
   parsley, and extra to garnish
2 onions, chopped
2 cloves garlic, crushed
⅓ cup (40 g/1¼ oz) plain flour
2½ cups (625 ml/21 fl oz) chicken
   stock
1 cup (250 ml/8 fl oz) good red
   wine
¼ cup (60 g/2 oz) tomato paste

1 Toss the lamb in the seasoned
flour, shaking off the excess. Preheat
the oven to moderate 180°C
(350°F/Gas 4).
2 Heat the oil in a heavy-based pan.
In batches, brown the lamb well on
both sides over medium-high heat.
Remove from the heat, drain well on
paper towels, then transfer to a
greased, 3 litre capacity ovenproof
casserole dish. Top with the celery,
carrots, potatoes, thyme and parsley.
3 Cook the onion and garlic in the
same heavy-based pan, stirring over
medium heat for about 5–10
minutes, or until the onion is soft.
4 Add the flour and stir for 1 minute,
or until the onion is coated. Add the
remaining ingredients and stir until
the sauce boils and thickens. Pour the
sauce over the lamb and vegetables.
Bake, covered, for 1¼ hours, or until
the lamb is tender. Carefully remove
the string from the lamb; sprinkle
with extra parsley to serve.

NUTRITION PER SERVE
Protein 40 g; Fat 60 g; Carbohydrate 60 g;
Dietary Fibre 10 g; Cholesterol 120 mg;
4050 kJ (970 cal)

COOK'S FILE

Notes: A noisette is a round slice of
meat, cut from a boned loin and tied

with string to hold its shape. For this
recipe you could also use a boned leg
of lamb, cut into 3 cm (1¼ inch)
cubes.
• If baby carrots are not available,
use four sliced carrots instead.
Storage time: This dish keeps for up
to 2 days. Cover and refrigerate, and
reheat gently before serving.

*Add the lightly floured lamb to the hot oil
and brown well all over.*

*Add the stock, wine and tomato paste to
the softened onion mixture.*

TAGINE OF LAMB WITH QUINCE AND LEMON

Preparation time: 25 minutes
Total cooking time: 2 hours 10 minutes
Serves 4

1.5 kg (3 lb) boned shoulder of
  lamb, cut into 12 even pieces
1 onion, finely chopped
2 cloves garlic, crushed
1 cinnamon stick
1 teaspoon ground ginger
½ teaspoon saffron threads
1 large quince, peeled, seeded
  and cut into 12 pieces
¼ cup (60 ml/2 fl oz) honey
1 teaspoon ground cinnamon

½ preserved lemon
chopped parsley, for serving

1 Trim the lamb of excess fat and place in a large pan. Add the onion, garlic, cinnamon stick, ginger and saffron and enough cold water to cover. Slowly bring to the boil, stirring occasionally. Reduce the heat, cover and simmer for 45 minutes. Transfer the meat to a large casserole dish and set aside.
2 Add the quince, honey and ground cinnamon to the cooking liquid and simmer for 15 minutes, or until the quince is tender. Discard the cinnamon stick; remove the quince and add to the meat, reserving the liquid.

3 Preheat an oven to moderate 180°C (350°F/Gas 4). Boil the cooking liquid for 30 minutes, or until reduced by half, then pour over the meat and quince. Remove and discard the flesh from the lemon. Slice the rind thinly, then add to the meat. Cover and bake for 40 minutes, or until the meat is tender. Sprinkle with parsley to serve.

NUTRITION PER SERVE
Protein 80 g; Fat 15 g; Carbohydrate 20 g; Dietary Fibre 3 g; Cholesterol 250 mg; 2160 kJ (515 cal)

COOK'S FILE

Hint: As you work, place the peeled quince in water with a little lemon juice to prevent discolouring.

Add the onion, garlic, cinnamon stick, ginger, saffron and cold water to the lamb.

Add the quince, honey and ground cinnamon to the cooking liquid.

Remove and discard the flesh from the preserved lemon and slice the rind thinly.

IRISH STEW

Preparation time: 20 minutes
Total cooking time: 1 hour 15 minutes
Serves 4

8 lamb neck chops
4 thick rashers bacon, rind
    removed
30 g (1 oz) butter
1 kg (2 lb) potatoes, thickly
    sliced
3 carrots, sliced
3 onions, sliced into thick rounds
2 cups (500 ml/16 fl oz) beef or
    vegetable stock

sprigs of thyme or lemon thyme,
    to taste
chopped parsley, to garnish

1 Trim the chops of excess fat; cut the bacon into short strips. Melt the butter in a large heavy-based pan and brown the chops on both sides over high heat. Remove and set aside. Add the bacon to the pan and cook until crisp. Drain on paper towels.
2 Arrange half the potato, carrot and onion in a deep heavy-based pan. Season with cracked pepper, then add half the bacon. Layer the chops on top and cover with the remaining potato, carrot, onion and bacon. Add

the stock and thyme.
3 Cover and bring to the boil, then reduce the heat and simmer for about 1 hour, or until the lamb is tender. Serve sprinkled with parsley.

NUTRITION PER SERVE
Protein 40 g; Fat 15 g; Carbohydrate 40 g; Dietary Fibre 7 g; Cholesterol 110 mg; 1870 kJ (450 cal)

COOK'S FILE

Note: Irish stew is traditionally made from mutton, without potatoes or carrots. Adding vegetables makes a satisfying one-pot meal.

Brown the chops on both sides in the hot butter over high heat.

Arrange half the potato, carrot and onion in a deep, heavy-based pan.

When the layers are complete, add the stock and thyme.

TRADITIONAL LAMB SHANKS

Preparation time: 30 minutes
Total cooking time: 2 hours 25 minutes
Serves 4–6

8 lamb shanks
1 tablespoon olive oil
1 orange
1 large onion, sliced
4 cloves garlic
1 large carrot, cut into chunks
1 parsnip, cut into chunks
1 stick celery, cut into chunks
2 bay leaves
3 cups (750 ml/24 fl oz) chicken
　stock
2 cups (500 ml/16 fl oz) red wine
1 tablespoon redcurrant jelly
3 teaspoons cornflour
sprigs of thyme, to garnish

1 Preheat the oven to warm 160°C (315°F/Gas 2–3). Pat the shanks dry with paper towels. Heat the oil in a flameproof casserole or baking dish large enough to fit the shanks in a single layer, then brown the shanks over high heat for 3 minutes, turning frequently. Remove and set aside.
2 Peel three 5 cm (2 inch) strips of rind from the orange, avoiding the bitter white pith. Set aside.
3 Add the onion and garlic cloves to the dish and cook over medium heat for 2 minutes, stirring. Add the carrot, parsnip and celery and place the shanks snugly on top. Add the rind strips and bay leaves, then pour in the stock and red wine. Cover and bake for 2 hours, or until the meat is very tender and comes away from the bone.
4 Using tongs, carefully remove the shanks from the dish; cover with foil to keep warm. Remove the rind and bay leaves and strain the juices into a pan. Set the vegetables aside.
5 Add the redcurrant jelly to the dish and stir to dissolve. Boil rapidly for 20 minutes, or until the sauce is reduced to 1½ cups (375 ml/12 fl oz). Combine the cornflour with a little water and whisk into the sauce, stirring until thickened and glossy.
6 To serve, place the lamb shanks on serving plates, arrange the vegetables on top, drizzle with the sauce and garnish with thyme.

NUTRITION PER SERVE (6)
Protein 40 g; Fat 7 g; Carbohydrate 9 g; Dietary Fibre 2.5 g; Cholesterol 112 mg; 1355 kJ (325 cal)

C O O K ' S　F I L E
Note: This recipe can be made 2 days ahead, or frozen for up to 2 months.

Heat the oil in a baking dish and brown the shanks over high heat.

Peel strips of rind from the orange, avoiding the bitter white pith.

LAMB'S LIVER AND BACON STEW

Preparation time: 10 minutes
Total cooking time: 30 minutes
Serves 6

1 lamb's liver, about 750 g (1½ lb)
¼ cup (30 g/1 oz) cornflour
¼ teaspoon ground black pepper
6 rashers bacon, cut into large pieces
2 tablespoons oil
2 onions, thinly sliced
1 beef stock cube, crumbled

1 Wash the liver and cut it into thin slices, discarding any veins or discoloured spots. Pat the liver dry with paper towels. Combine the cornflour and pepper. Toss the liver slices in the seasoned cornflour, shaking off the excess.
2 Cook the bacon in a heavy-based saucepan until crisp, then drain on paper towels. Heat the oil in the pan and cook the onion gently until golden, then remove from the pan.
3 Cook the liver quickly in small batches over medium heat until well browned, then drain on paper towels. Return the liver, bacon and onion to the pan. Dissolve the stock cube in 1 cup (250 ml/8 fl oz) boiling water, then gradually add to the pan. Stir over medium heat for 10 minutes, or until the liquid boils and thickens. Serve the stew immediately.

NUTRITION PER SERVE
Protein 36 g; Fat 30 g; Carbohydrate 9 g; Dietary Fibre 0.5 g; Cholesterol 573 mg; 1850 kJ (440 cal)

NOTE: Soaking the liver in milk for 30 minutes before cooking will result in a milder taste.

Toss the liver slices in the seasoned cornflour, shaking off the excess.

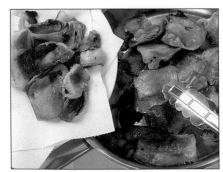

Cook the bacon in a heavy-based saucepan until crisp, then drain on paper towels.

Return the cooked bacon, liver slices and onion to the pan.

LAMB WITH BORLOTTI BEANS

Preparation time: 20 minutes +
overnight soaking
Total cooking time: 2 hours
Serves 6

1 cup (200 g /6½ oz) dried
   borlotti beans
1 tablespoon olive oil
12 lamb loin chops
1 onion, finely chopped
1 stick celery, chopped
1 carrot, chopped
3 cloves garlic, finely chopped
½ teaspoon dried chilli flakes
1 teaspoon cumin seeds
2 cups (500 ml/16 fl oz) lamb or
   chicken stock
2 bay leaves
3 tablespoons lemon juice
⅓ cup (20 g/¾ oz) chopped
   parsley
1 tablespoon shredded mint

1 Soak the beans overnight in cold water. Drain, rinse well and set aside.
2 Preheat the oven to moderate 180°C (350°F/Gas 4). Heat the oil in a large heavy-based pan. Brown the lamb over high heat in batches and transfer to a casserole dish.
3 Add the onion, celery and carrot to the pan and cook over low heat for about 10 minutes, or until soft and golden. Add the garlic, chilli and cumin seeds and cook for 1 minute, then transfer to the casserole dish.
4 Add the stock, beans and bay leaves. Cover tightly; bake for 10–1¾ hours, or until the lamb is very tender and the beans are cooked. Season with salt and freshly cracked black pepper. Stir in the lemon juice, parsley and mint just before serving.

NUTRITION PER SERVE
Protein 30 g; Fat 8 g; Carbohydrate 20 g;
Dietary Fibre 5 g; Cholesterol 65 mg;
1185 kJ (280 cal)

When the oil is hot, brown the lamb over high heat in batches.

Add the onion, celery and carrot to the pan and cook until soft and golden.

Add the stock, drained borlotti beans and bay leaves to the casserole.

LAMB AND MUSTARD STEW

Preparation time: 15 minutes
Total cooking time: 1 hour 40 minutes
Serves 4

750 g (1½ lb) lean lamb fillets,
    cut into 2.5 cm (1 inch) cubes
½ cup (60 g/2 oz) plain flour
1 tablespoon oil
16 baby onions
1 cup (250 ml/8 fl oz) white wine

1 cup (250 ml/8 fl oz) chicken
    stock
½ cup (125 g/4 oz) Dijon mustard
2 tablespoons chopped fresh thyme

1 Toss the lamb cubes in the flour, shaking off any excess. Heat the oil in a heavy-based saucepan over high heat. Add the lamb in small batches and cook for 3 minutes, or until well browned, turning occasionally. Drain on paper towels.
2 Return the lamb to the pan. Add the onions, wine, stock, mustard and thyme. Bring to the boil, then reduce the heat to low and simmer, covered, for 1 hour, stirring occasionally. Remove the lid and simmer for another 30 minutes, or until the lamb is tender. Serve with pasta.

NUTRITION PER SERVE
Protein 46 g; Fat 11 g; Carbohydrate 18 g;
Dietary Fibre 2.5 g; Cholesterol 124 mg;
1655 kJ (395 cal)

NOTE: A small, boned leg of lamb is ideal for this dish.

Toss the lamb cubes in the flour, shaking off any excess flour.

Brown the lamb in small batches, turning occasionally, then drain on paper towels.

Add the onions, wine, stock, mustard and thyme to the pan.

10

LAMB AND SPINACH CURRY

Preparation time: 30 minutes
Total cooking time: 2 hours 20 minutes
Serves 6

1 kg (2 lb) English spinach
½ cup (125 ml/4 fl oz) oil
1.5 kg (3 lb) lamb, cut into 3 cm
   (1¼ inch) cubes
2 red onions, finely chopped
6 cloves garlic, crushed
1½ tablespoons grated fresh
   ginger
2 bay leaves
2 tablespoons ground coriander
1 tablespoon ground cumin
1 teaspoon ground turmeric
2 large vine-ripened tomatoes,
   peeled, seeded and chopped
2–3 small fresh green chillies,
   seeded and finely chopped
100 g (3½ oz) plain thick yoghurt
1 cinnamon stick
2 teaspoons garam masala

1 Preheat the oven to warm 170°C (325°F/Gas 3). Trim the spinach and quickly blanch in simmering water. Drain, cool slightly and squeeze to remove any excess moisture, then place in a food processor and process until smooth.

2 Heat half the oil in a large saucepan. Add the lamb pieces in batches and cook over high heat for 4–5 minutes, or until browned. Remove the lamb from the pan.

3 Heat the remaining oil in the saucepan. Add the onion and cook, stirring frequently, for 10 minutes, or until golden brown but not burnt. Add the garlic, ginger and bay leaves, and cook, stirring, for 3 more minutes.

4 Add the spices and cook, stirring, for 2 minutes, or until fragrant. Add the tomato and chilli, and stir over low heat for 5 minutes, or until the tomato is thick and pulpy. Remove from the heat and cool for 5 minutes. Transfer to a 4 litre casserole dish and stir in the yoghurt.

5 Return the meat to the dish and add the cinnamon stick and 1 teaspoon salt. Bake, covered, for 1 hour and then uncovered for a further 15 minutes. Stir in the spinach and garam masala, and cook,

stirring occasionally, for 15 minutes, or until the meat is tender. Remove the bay leaves and cinnamon stick, and serve with rice or pilaf.

NUTRITION PER SERVE
Protein 60 g; Fat 30 g; Carbohydrate 5 g; Dietary Fibre 6.5 g; Cholesterol 170 mg; 2240 kJ (533 cal)

NOTE: Ask your butcher to bone and cut the lamb for you. A 2.2 kg (4 lb 6½ oz) leg will yield about 1.5 kg (3 lb) meat.

Squeeze the blanched spinach to remove any excess moisture.

Process the cooked spinach in a food processor until smooth.

Stir in the tomato and chilli over low heat until the tomato is thick and pulpy.

ROSEMARY-INFUSED LAMB AND LENTIL CASSEROLE

Preparation time: 20 minutes
Total cooking time: 2 hours 30 minutes
Serves 6

25 g (¾ oz) butter
2 tablespoons olive oil
1 onion, finely sliced
2 cloves garlic, crushed
1 small carrot, finely chopped
2 teaspoons cumin seeds
¼ teaspoon chilli flakes
2 teaspoons finely chopped fresh
  ginger
1 kg (2 lb) boned leg of lamb, cut
  into 4 cm (1½ inch) cubes
2 teaspoons rosemary leaves
3 cups (750 ml/24 fl oz) lamb or
  chicken stock
1 cup (185 g/6 oz) green or brown
  lentils
3 teaspoons soft brown sugar
2 teaspoons balsamic vinegar
sprigs of rosemary, to garnish

1 Preheat the oven to moderate 180°C (350°F/Gas 4). Heat the butter and half the oil in a large, heavy-based pan. Add the onion, garlic and carrot and cook over medium heat for about 5 minutes, or until soft and golden. Add the cumin seeds, chilli flakes and ginger, cook for 1 minute, then transfer to a large casserole dish.
2 Heat the remaining oil in the pan and brown the lamb in batches over high heat. Transfer to the casserole dish.
3 Add the rosemary to the pan and stir in 2½ cups (625 ml/20 fl oz) of the stock, scraping up all the brown bits from the base and side of the

pan. Heat until the stock is bubbling, then pour into the casserole dish. Cover and bake for 1 hour.
4 Add the lentils, sugar and vinegar and cook for 1 hour more, or until the lentils are cooked. If the mixture is too thick, stir in the remaining

stock. Season with salt and freshly ground pepper and garnish with rosemary sprigs to serve.

NUTRITION PER SERVE
Protein 45 g; Fat 15 g; Carbohydrate 15 g; Dietary Fibre 5 g; Cholesterol 120 mg; 1618 kJ (385 cal)

When the oil is hot, add the onion, garlic and carrot and cook until soft and golden.

After browning the lamb, add the rosemary and stock, scraping up the brown bits.

Bake the casserole for 1 hour, then add the lentils, sugar and vinegar.

LAMB STEW WITH ROSEMARY DUMPLINGS

Preparation time: 25 minutes
Total cooking time: 2 hours
Serves 4

8 lamb neck chops
plain flour, seasoned with salt
    and freshly ground pepper
2 tablespoons oil
2 rashers bacon, finely chopped
1 large onion, sliced
2 cups (500 ml/16 fl oz) beef
    stock
1 tablespoon chopped thyme
2 carrots, thickly sliced
2 potatoes, chopped

Rosemary Dumplings
1 cup (125 g/4 oz) self-raising
    flour
20 g (¾ oz) butter, chopped
1 tablespoon chopped rosemary
⅓ cup (80 ml/2¾ fl oz) milk

1 Trim the lamb of fat and sinew and toss lightly in the flour, shaking off any excess. Heat the oil in a large, heavy-based pan, then brown the lamb in batches over medium-high heat. Remove and set aside.
2 Add the bacon to the pan and cook over medium heat for 2 minutes, or until brown. Add the onion and cook for about 5 minutes, or until soft.
3 Return the browned lamb to the pan. Add the stock, thyme and ½ cup (125 ml/4 fl oz) of water, then simmer, covered, over low heat for 30 minutes. Add the carrot and potato and simmer for 1 hour more.
4 To make the rosemary dumplings, sift the flour into a bowl, then rub in the butter with your fingertips until

the mixture is fine and crumbly. Mix in the rosemary. Add most of the milk and mix to a soft dough with a knife, adding more milk if needed. Turn out onto a lightly floured surface and gently knead until smooth. Divide the dough into 12 portions and form into rough balls. Place the dumplings on top of the stew, then cover and cook for 15 minutes. Serve immediately.

NUTRITION PER SERVE
Protein 30 g; Fat 20 g; Carbohydrate 35 g; Dietary Fibre 4 g; Cholesterol 95 mg; 1930 kJ (460 cal)

C O O K ' S   F I L E
Storage time: The stew may be made a day ahead, but the dumplings should be made just before serving. Simply reheat the stew to simmering point, then add the fresh dumplings.

Lightly toss the trimmed lamb in the seasoned flour, shaking off any excess.

Sift the flour into a bowl. Rub in the butter with your fingertips until fine.

Divide the dough into 12 portions, then form into rough balls.

LANCASHIRE HOTPOT

Preparation time: 20 minutes
Total cooking time: 2 hours
Serves 8

8 lamb forequarter chops
4 lamb's kidneys
¼ cup (30 g/1 oz) plain flour
50 g (1¾ oz) butter
4 potatoes, thinly sliced
2 large brown onions, sliced
1 large carrot, chopped
1¾ cups (440 ml/14 fl oz) beef or
vegetable stock
2 teaspoons chopped fresh thyme
1 bay leaf
melted butter, extra

1 Preheat the oven to warm 160°C (315°F/Gas 2–3), and grease a large casserole dish. Trim the chops of excess fat and sinew, then remove the cores from the kidneys and cut into quarters. Toss the chops and kidneys in the flour, shaking off and reserving the excess. Heat the butter in a frying pan and brown the chops quickly on both sides. Remove the chops from the pan and brown the kidneys.
2 Layer half the potato slices in the base of the casserole and top with the chops and kidneys.
3 Add the onion and carrot to the pan, and cook until the carrot begins to brown. Layer on top of the chops and kidneys. Sprinkle the reserved flour over the base of the pan and fry, stirring, until dark brown. Gradually pour in the stock and bring to the boil, stirring. Season well, and add the thyme and bay leaf. Reduce the heat and simmer for 10 minutes. Pour into the casserole dish.
4 Layer the remaining potato over the meat and vegetables. Cover and bake for 1¼ hours. Increase the oven temperature to moderate 180°C (350°F/Gas 4), brush the potato with the extra melted butter and cook, uncovered, for 20 minutes, or until the potato is brown.

NUTRITION PER SERVE
Protein 38 g; Fat 11 g; Carbohydrate 13 g; Dietary Fibre 2 g; Cholesterol 175 mg; 1285 kJ (305 cal)

Remove the cores from the kidneys and then cut the kidneys into quarters.

Cover the base with potato slices, then add the chops and kidneys.

Layer the remaining potato slices over the meat and vegetables.

LAMB AND BEAN CASSEROLE

Preparation time: 25 minutes +
  overnight soaking
Total cooking time: 2 hours 15 minutes
Serves 6

1½ cups (300 g/10 oz) borlotti
  beans or red kidney beans
1 kg (2 lb) boned leg of lamb
1½ tablespoons olive oil
2 rashers bacon, rind removed,
  chopped
1 large onion, chopped
2 cloves garlic, crushed
1 large carrot, chopped
2 cups (500 ml/16 fl oz) dry red
  wine
1 tablespoon tomato paste

1½ cups (375 ml/12 fl oz) beef
  stock
2 large sprigs fresh rosemary
2 sprigs fresh thyme

1 Put the beans in a bowl and cover with plenty of water. Leave to soak overnight, then drain well.
2 Preheat the oven to warm 160°C (315°F/Gas 2–3). Trim any excess fat from the lamb and cut the lamb into 3 cm (1¼ inch) pieces.
3 Heat 1 tablespoon oil in a large flameproof casserole dish. Add half the meat and toss over medium–high heat for 2 minutes, or until browned. Remove from the casserole and repeat with the remaining lamb. Remove from the casserole.
4 Heat the remaining olive oil in the casserole and add the bacon and onion. Cook over medium heat for 3 minutes, or until the onion is translucent. Add the garlic and carrot, and cook for 1 minute, or until the mixture is aromatic.
5 Return the meat and any juices to the casserole, increase the heat to high and add the wine. Bring to the boil and cook for 2 minutes. Add the beans, tomato paste, stock, rosemary and thyme, return to the boil, then cover and bake for 2 hours, or until the meat is tender. Stir occasionally during cooking. Skim off any excess fat, remove the sprigs of herbs, and season. Serve with bread.

NUTRITION PER SERVE
Protein 50 g; Fat 10 g; Carbohydrate 48 g; Dietary Fibre 9 g; Cholesterol 117 mg; 2367 kJ (565 cal)

Remove any excess fat from the lamb, then cut it into large pieces.

Heat the oil, then add the lamb and toss until it is browned all over.

Return the meat and juices to the casserole dish, add the wine and bring to the boil.

KIDNEYS IN CREAMY MUSTARD SAUCE

Preparation time: 15 minutes
Total cooking time: 25 minutes
Serves 4

8 lamb kidneys
50 g (1¾ oz) butter
6 French shallots, finely sliced
1 cup (250 ml/8 fl oz) cream
2 teaspoons wholegrain mustard
2 teaspoons Dijon mustard
⅓ cup (20 g/¾ oz) chopped
  parsley

1 To prepare the kidneys, slice them in half lengthways. Using a pair of small sharp scissors, carefully snip out the core of each kidney and remove any membrane.
2 Melt half the butter in a small pan. Add the shallots and gently cook for 5 minutes, or until soft and golden. Add the cream and simmer for 10 minutes, or until reduced by one-quarter. Remove from the heat and stir in both mustards; mix well and set aside.
3 Melt the remaining butter in a frying pan over medium heat. When the butter foams, cook the kidney halves for 2 minutes on each side.

4 Pour the creamy mustard sauce over the kidneys and simmer, stirring, for 2 minutes. Stir in the chopped parsley and serve.

NUTRITION PER SERVE
Protein 20 g; Fat 40 g; Carbohydrate 2 g; Dietary Fibre 0 g; Cholesterol 455 mg; 1820 kJ (435 cal)

COOK'S FILE

NOTE: When buying kidneys, select those that are firm and have a rich, even colour.
Serving suggestion: This dish is delicious served with mashed potato and steamed green beans.

Cut the kidneys in half lengthways and remove the core and membrane.

Add the two mustards to the cream and stir until well combined.

Pour the cream and mustard sauce over the kidneys.

MOROCCAN LAMB SHANKS

Preparation time: 25 minutes
Total cooking time: 3 hours 15 minutes
Serves 4

Spicy Paste
30 g (1 oz) bunch coriander, roots intact
1 teaspoon ground turmeric
2 teaspoons ground cumin
1 teaspoon paprika
1 teaspoon ground coriander
½ teaspoon ground cinnamon
1 dried red chilli
2 cloves garlic, crushed
2 tablespoons honey
¼ cup (60 ml/2 fl oz) olive oil

light olive oil, for cooking
8 lamb shanks
3 onions, sliced into thick rings
sugar, for sprinkling
1 cup (250 ml/8 fl oz) white wine
2 cups (500 ml/16 fl oz) chicken stock
4 lime quarters, to garnish
coriander leaves, to garnish

1 In a food processor, blend the spicy paste ingredients (including coriander roots) to a smooth paste. Set aside.
2 Heat 3 tablespoons of oil in a large, heavy-based pan. Brown the shanks in batches over high heat and transfer to a large, ovenproof dish. Preheat the oven to moderate 180°C (350°F/Gas 4).
3 Heat a tablespoon of oil in the pan. Add the onion rings, sprinkle with sugar and sauté over medium heat for 10–15 minutes, or until golden.
4 Add the spicy paste and sauté for 2 minutes. Season well, add the wine and stock and simmer for 15 minutes.
5 Pour the wine sauce over the lamb shanks. Cover and bake for 1 hour, then turn the shanks over and bake for another 1½ hours, or until the meat is tender. Spoon any fat from the surface, transfer to plates and garnish with lime quarters and coriander leaves. Serve with couscous.

NUTRITION PER SERVE
Protein 60 g; Fat 20 g; Carbohydrate 15 g; Dietary Fibre 2 g; Cholesterol 170 mg; 2214 kJ (530 cal)

Blend all the spicy paste ingredients in a food processor until smooth.

Heat the oil in a large pan. Brown the shanks over high heat.

Add the spicy paste to the fried onion and sauté for 2 minutes.

LAMB ROGAN JOSH

Preparation time: 25 minutes
Total cooking time: 1 hour 40 minutes
Serves 4–6

1 tablespoon ghee or oil
2 onions, chopped
½ cup (125 g/4 oz) plain yoghurt
1 teaspoon chilli powder
1 tablespoon ground coriander
2 teaspoons ground cumin
1 teaspoon ground cardamom
½ teaspoon ground cloves
1 teaspoon ground turmeric
3 cloves garlic, crushed
1 tablespoon grated fresh ginger

400 g (13 oz) can chopped
   tomatoes
1 kg (2 lb) boned leg of lamb, cut
   into 2.5 cm (1 inch) cubes
¼ cup (30 g/1 oz) slivered almonds
1 teaspoon garam masala
chopped fresh coriander leaves,
   to garnish

1 Heat the ghee in a large saucepan, add the onion and cook, stirring, for 5 minutes, or until soft. Stir in the yoghurt, chilli powder, coriander, cumin, cardamom, cloves, turmeric, garlic and ginger. Add the tomato and 1 teaspoon salt, and simmer for 5 minutes.
2 Add the lamb and stir until coated.

Cover and cook over low heat, stirring occasionally, for 1–1½ hours, or until the lamb is tender. Uncover and simmer until the liquid thickens.
3 Meanwhile, toast the almonds in a dry frying pan over medium heat for 3–4 minutes, shaking the pan gently, until the nuts are golden brown. Remove from the pan.
4 Add the garam masala to the curry and mix through well. Sprinkle the slivered almonds and coriander leaves over the top, and serve.

NUTRITION PER SERVE (6)
Protein 40 g; Fat 13 g; Carbohydrate 5.5 g; Dietary Fibre 2 g; Cholesterol 122 mg; 1236 kJ (295 cal)

Cook the onion in the ghee for 5 minutes, or until the onion is soft.

Remove the lid and simmer the curry until the liquid thickens.

Toast the almonds in a dry frying pan over medium heat, shaking the pan gently.

LAMB HOTPOT WITH RICE NOODLES

Preparation time: 20 minutes + 2 hours marinating
Total cooking time: 2 hours
Serves 4

2 cloves garlic, crushed
2 teaspoons grated fresh ginger
1 teaspoon five-spice powder
¼ teaspoon ground white pepper
2 tablespoons Chinese rice wine
1 teaspoon sugar
1 kg (2 lb) boneless lamb shoulder, trimmed and cut into 3 cm (1¼ inch) pieces
30 g (1 oz) whole dried Chinese mushrooms
1 tablespoon peanut oil
1 large onion, cut into wedges
2 cm (¾ inch) piece fresh ginger, julienned
1 teaspoon Sichuan peppercorns, crushed or ground
2 tablespoons sweet bean paste
1 teaspoon black peppercorns, ground and toasted
2 cups (500 ml/16 fl oz) chicken stock
¼ cup (60 ml/2 fl oz) oyster sauce
2 star anise
¼ cup (60 ml/2 fl oz) Chinese rice wine, extra
80 g (2¾ oz) can sliced bamboo shoots
100 g (3½ oz) can water chestnuts, drained and sliced
400 g (13 oz) fresh rice noodles, cut into 2 cm (¾ inch) wide strips
1 spring onion, sliced on the diagonal

1 Combine the garlic, grated ginger, five-spice powder, white pepper, rice wine, sugar and 1 teaspoon salt in a large bowl. Add the lamb and toss to coat. Cover and marinate for 2 hours.
2 Meanwhile, soak the mushrooms in boiling water for 20 minutes. Drain. Discard the stems and slice the caps.
3 Heat a wok over high heat, add the oil and swirl to coat. Stir-fry the onion, julienned ginger and Sichuan pepper for 2 minutes. Cook the lamb in three batches, stir-frying for 2–3 minutes each batch, or until starting to brown. Return all the lamb to the

wok. Stir in the bean paste and black peppercorns, and cook for 3 minutes, or until the lamb is brown.
4 Add the stock and transfer to a 2 litre flameproof clay pot or casserole dish. Stir in the oyster sauce, star anise and extra rice wine and simmer, covered, over low heat for 1½ hours, or until the lamb is tender. Stir in the drained bamboo shoots and water chestnuts, and cook for 20 minutes. Add the mushrooms.

5 Cover the noodles with boiling water and gently separate. Drain and rinse the noodles, then add to the hotpot, stirring for 1–2 minutes, or until heated through. Serve sprinkled with spring onion.

NUTRITION PER SERVE
Protein 58 g; Fat 21 g; Carbohydrate 57 g; Dietary Fibre 4 g; Cholesterol 168 mg; 2805 kJ (670 cal)

Stir the bean paste and peppercorns into the lamb and onion mixture.

Stir the bamboo shoots and water chestnuts into the hotpot.

BEEF AND RED WINE STEW

Preparation time: 15 minutes
Total cooking time: 2 hours
Serves 6

30 g (1 oz) butter
2 tablespoons oil
1 kg (2 lb) topside steak,
    trimmed and cut into 3 cm
    (1¼ inch) cubes
100 g (3½ oz) bacon pieces, cut
    into 1.5 cm (5/8 inch) cubes
18 baby onions
2 cloves garlic, crushed
¼ cup (30 g/1 oz) plain flour
2 cups (500 ml/16 fl oz) red wine
3 cups (750 ml/24 fl oz) beef
    stock
300 g (10 oz) small mushrooms,
    halved

1 Heat the butter and oil in a heavy-based saucepan. Cook the meat quickly in small batches over medium–high heat until browned, then drain on paper towels.
2 Add the bacon, onions and garlic to the pan, and cook, stirring, for 2 minutes, or until browned. Add the flour and stir over low heat until lightly golden. Gradually pour in the wine and stock, and stir until smooth. Stir continuously over medium heat for 2 minutes, or until the mixture boils and thickens.
3 Return the meat to the pan and reduce the heat to a simmer. Cook, covered, for 1½ hours, or until the meat is tender, stirring occasionally. Add the mushrooms and cook for 15 minutes. Delicious served with mashed potato.

NUTRITION PER SERVE
Protein 45 g; Fat 17 g; Carbohydrate 10 g; Dietary Fibre 2.5 g; Cholesterol 105 mg; 1800 kJ (430 cal)

Using a large sharp knife, cut the topside steak into large cubes.

Cook the meat in small batches until browned, then drain on paper towels.

Add the flour to the bacon, onions and garlic, and stir until lightly golden.

When the meat is tender, add the halved mushrooms to the pan.

SPICY BEEF, POTATO AND CAPSICUM STEW

Preparation time: 35 minutes
Total cooking time: 2 hours 20 minutes
Serves 4–6

300 g (10 oz) French shallots
2 tablespoons olive oil
1 kg (2 lb) gravy beef, cut into 4 cm (1¼ inch) cubes
4 cloves garlic, crushed
3 teaspoons paprika
1 teaspoon fennel seeds
½ teaspoon ground cumin
1 tablespoon plain flour
½ cup (125 ml/4 fl oz) red wine
2 tablespoons brandy
½ teaspoon dried thyme
½ teaspoon dried oregano
1 bay leaf
1½ cups (375 ml/12 fl oz) beef stock
1 tablespoon honey
400 g (13 oz) potatoes, cut into large chunks
2 red capsicums, chopped
½ cup (125 g/4 oz) sour cream
chopped chives, for serving

1 Preheat the oven to moderate 180°C (350°F/Gas 4). Place the shallots in a bowl, cover with boiling water and leave for 30 seconds. Drain and peel.

2 Heat the oil in a large, heavy-based pan, then brown the meat in batches over medium-high heat and transfer to a large casserole dish.

3 Add the shallots to the pan and cook over medium heat until soft and golden. Add the garlic, paprika, fennel seeds and cumin; cook until fragrant.

4 Add the flour, cook for 30 seconds, then remove from the heat. Stir in the red wine and brandy. Return to the heat and add the thyme, oregano, bay leaf and stock. Stir until the mixture bubbles, then add to the meat.

5 Cover and bake for 1½ hours, then add the honey, potato and capsicum. Cook, uncovered, for 30 minutes, or until the potato is tender. Season to taste. Serve with a dollop of sour cream and a sprinkling of chives.

NUTRITION PER SERVE (6)
Protein 40 g; Fat 20 g; Carbohydrate 30 g; Dietary Fibre 3 g; Cholesterol 140 mg; 1790 kJ (430 cal)

Remove the skin from the blanched and drained shallots.

Brown the meat in batches in the hot oil over medium-high heat.

Add the red wine and brandy to the spice mixture and stir well.

BEEF POT ROAST PROVENCALE

Preparation time: 15 minutes
Total cooking time: 2 hours 15 minutes
Serves 6

2 tablespoons oil
2 kg (4 lb) rolled beef brisket, trimmed
3 cups (750 ml/24 fl oz) beef stock
1 cup (250 ml/8 fl oz) red wine
¼ cup (60 ml/2 fl oz) brandy
2 onions, quartered
3 cloves garlic, crushed

3 tomatoes, peeled, seeded and chopped
2 bay leaves
¼ cup (15 g/½ oz) chopped fresh parsley
2 tablespoons fresh thyme leaves
12 pitted black olives
6 small carrots, thickly sliced
2 tablespoons plain flour

1 Heat the oil in a deep heavy-based saucepan. Cook the meat over medium–high heat until browned all over, then remove from the heat.
2 Add the stock to the pan with the wine, brandy, onion, garlic, tomato, bay leaves, parsley and thyme. Cover and bring to simmering point over low heat. Simmer for 1½ hours.
3 Add the olives and carrot, and cook for 30 minutes. Remove the meat and leave it in a warm place, covered with foil, for 10 minutes before slicing.
4 Combine the flour and ¼ cup (60 ml/2 fl oz) water to make a smooth paste. Add to the sauce, stir over medium heat until the sauce thickens, and cook for 3 minutes. Pour over the sliced meat to serve.

NUTRITION PER SERVE
Protein 70 g; Fat 11 g; Carbohydrate 11.5 g; Dietary Fibre 2.5 g; Cholesterol 150 mg; 2005 kJ (480 cal)

Cook the meat in the oil over medium–high heat until it is browned all over.

Add the stock to the pan with the wine, brandy, onion, garlic, tomato and herbs.

Add the olives and carrot to the pan, and cook for 30 minutes.

SMOKED SAUSAGE AND KIDNEY BEAN STEW

Preparation time: 20 minutes
Total cooking time: 2 hours 30 minutes
Serves 4–6

1 small red capsicum, halved
2 tablespoons olive oil
2–3 cloves garlic, crushed
1 large onion, thinly sliced
1 carrot, cut into cubes
420 g (14 oz) can kidney beans,
    rinsed and drained
2 cups (500 ml/16 fl oz) beef
    stock
1 tablespoon treacle
600 g (1¼ lb) piece speck or
    bacon
425 g (14 oz) can chopped
    tomatoes, juice reserved
2 tablespoons tomato paste
150 g (5 oz) smoked sausages

1 Grill the capsicum halves, skin-side-up, under a hot grill until the skin is black and blistered. Cool, then peel off the skin and dice the flesh.
2 Heat the oil in a large, heavy-based pan. Add the garlic, onion and carrot and cook, stirring, over low heat for 4–5 minutes without browning.
3 Add the beans, stock, treacle and freshly ground black pepper to taste. Slowly bring to the boil, then add the speck or bacon. Reduce the heat; cover and simmer for 1 hour. Stir through the undrained tomatoes and tomato paste and simmer for 30 minutes.
4 Place the sausages in a pan of cold water. Slowly bring to the boil, then drain and add to the stew. Simmer, uncovered, for 45 minutes, or until the sauce is thick and rich.

5 Remove the speck or bacon and sausages, using tongs. Slice them, removing any fat and skin, and return to the stew for serving. Serve hot.

NUTRITION PER SERVE (6)
Protein 25 g; Fat 15 g; Carbohydrate 20 g; Dietary Fibre 8 g; Cholesterol 50 mg; 1370 kJ (330 cal)

COOK'S FILE

Note: Speck is a kind of smoked bacon, often sold in delicatessens.
Serving suggestion: This stew is lovely with a Pumpkin and white bean purée.

Add the beans, stock, treacle and pepper to the onion mixture.

Simmer the stew until rich and thick, then remove the speck and sausages.

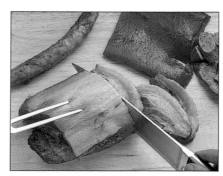

Remove the skin and excess fat from the speck. Slice the sausages and speck.

RICH STEAK AND KIDNEY STEW

Preparation time: 35 minutes
Total cooking time: 2 hours 30 minutes
Serves 4–6

1 kg (2 lb) chuck steak, trimmed
8 lamb kidneys
¼ cup (60 ml/2 fl oz) oil
1 rasher bacon, rind removed,
    and cut into long, thin strips
40 g (1¼ oz) butter
1 large onion, chopped
300 g (10 oz) button mushrooms,
    halved
1 cup (250 ml/8 fl oz) Muscat
2–3 cloves garlic, crushed
¼ teaspoon ground allspice
½ teaspoon paprika
2 teaspoons coriander seeds,
    lightly crushed
1 tablespoon wholegrain mustard
1 cup (250 ml/8 fl oz) beef stock
2–3 tablespoons soft brown sugar
1–2 teaspoons thyme
1–2 teaspoons rosemary

1 Cut the steak into 2–3 cm (1 inch) cubes. Cut the kidneys in half, remove the core and fat, then slice them in half again.
2 Heat 1 teaspoon of the oil in a large, heavy-based pan. Add the bacon and cook over medium heat until just crisp. Remove and set aside.
3 Heat 2 tablespoons of the oil and 30 g (1 oz) of the butter in the pan. Brown the steak in batches and set aside.
4 Add the onion to the pan and cook for 3 minutes, or until soft and golden. Add the mushrooms and cook, stirring, for 3 minutes, until starting to brown. Stir in half the Muscat and simmer for 3–4 minutes. Remove and set aside.
5 Add the remaining oil and butter to the pan. Stir in the garlic, allspice, paprika and coriander and cook for 1 minute. Add the kidneys and cook until just starting to brown. Stir in the mustard and remaining Muscat and simmer for 2 minutes.
6 Stir in the bacon, steak, onion and mushrooms. Stir in the stock, bring to the boil, then reduce the heat, cover and simmer for 1 hour. Add the sugar.
7 Simmer, covered, for 40 minutes, then uncovered for 20 minutes, stirring in the herbs during the last 10 minutes.

NUTRITION PER SERVE (6)
Protein 40 g; Fat 20 g; Carbohydrate 15 g; Dietary Fibre 2 g; Cholesterol 155 mg; 1830 kJ (440 cal)

Halve the kidneys and remove the cores and fat. Slice in half again.

Add half the Muscat to the onions and mushrooms and simmer for 3–4 minutes.

Add the kidneys to the pan-fried spices and cook until just starting to brown.

24

MEXICAN BEEF STEW

Preparation time: 30 minutes
Total cooking time: 1 hour 30 minutes
Serves 6

500 g (1 lb) Roma tomatoes,
   halved
6 flour tortillas
1–2 fresh red chillies, finely
   chopped
1 tablespoon olive oil
1 kg (2 lb) stewing beef, cubed
½ teaspoon black pepper
2 onions, thinly sliced
1½ cups (375 ml/12 fl oz) beef
   stock
¼ cup (60 g/2 oz) tomato paste

375 g (12 oz) can kidney beans,
   drained
1 teaspoon chilli powder
½ cup (125 g/4 oz) sour cream

1 Preheat the oven to moderate 180°C (350°F/Gas 4). Grill the tomatoes, skin-side up, under a hot grill for 6–8 minutes, or until the skin is black and blistered. Cool, remove the skin and roughly chop the flesh.
2 Bake 2 of the tortillas for 4 minutes, or until crisp. Break into pieces and put in a food processor with the tomato and chilli. Process for 30 seconds, or until almost smooth.
3 Heat the oil in a large heavy-based saucepan. Brown the beef in batches, season with pepper, then remove. Add the onion to the pan and cook for 5 minutes. Return the meat to the pan. Stir in the processed mixture, stock and tomato paste, and bring to the boil. Reduce the heat, cover and simmer for 1¼ hours. Add the beans and chilli powder, and heat through.
4 Grill the remaining tortillas for 2–3 minutes on each side, then cool and cut into wedges. Serve the stew with the sour cream, and toasted tortilla wedges on the side.

NUTRITION PER SERVE
Protein 50 g; Fat 20 g; Carbohydrate 40 g; Dietary Fibre 8 g; Cholesterol 125 mg; 2235 kJ (535 cal)

Grill the tomatoes until the skin is black and blistered and it will peel away easily.

Once the tortillas are crisp, break into pieces and put in the food processor.

Stir the processed mixture, stock and tomato paste into the beef mixture.

25

BEEF SAUSAGE AND MUSHROOM STEW

Preparation time: 20 minutes + 30 minutes standing
Cooking time: 1 hour
Serves 4–6

15 g (½ oz) packet dried porcini mushrooms
12 thick beef sausages
300 g (10 oz) piece speck or bacon
2 teaspoons oil
2 onions, cut into eighths
8 cloves garlic
1 sprig of thyme
3 bay leaves
1½ cups (375 ml/12 fl oz) red wine

1 cup (250 ml/8 fl oz) beef stock
1 teaspoon Dijon mustard
1 bunch baby carrots
100 g (3½ oz) Swiss brown mushrooms, halved
100 g (3½ oz) button mushrooms, halved
1 tablespoon cornflour
chopped parsley, for serving

1 Soak the mushrooms for 30 minutes in enough boiling water to cover.
2 Brown the sausages well all over in a lightly oiled pan over medium heat. Drain on paper towels and place in a large, flameproof casserole dish.
3 Remove the rind from the speck or bacon; cut the meat into small strips. Heat the oil in a pan and add the speck, onions and garlic. Cook, stirring, until the onions are golden, then place in the casserole dish with the thyme, bay leaves, wine, stock and mustard. Cover, bring to the boil, then reduce the heat and simmer for 20 minutes.
4 Reserving 3 tablespoons of liquid, drain the mushrooms. Add the carrots and all mushrooms to the stew. Cover and simmer for 20 minutes. Mix the cornflour into the reserved liquid; stir into the stew until it boils and thickens. Sprinkle with parsley to serve.

NUTRITION PER SERVE (6)
Protein 30 g; Fat 40 g; Carbohydrate 10 g; Dietary Fibre 7 g; Cholesterol 115 mg; 2455 kJ (590 cal)

COOK'S FILE

NOTE: Speck is a type of smoked bacon sold in delicatessens.

Cover the porcini mushrooms with boiling water and soak for 30 minutes.

Remove the rind from the speck and cut the meat into small strips.

Add the carrots and all the mushrooms to the sausages. Simmer for 20 minutes.

BRAISED OXTAIL CASSEROLE

Preparation time: 15 minutes
Total cooking time: 2 hours
Serves 6

¼ cup (60 ml/2 fl oz) oil
16 small pieces oxtail, about 1.5 kg (3 lb)
4 baby potatoes, halved
1 large onion, chopped
2 carrots, chopped
250 g (8 oz) button mushrooms
2 tablespoons plain flour
3 cups (750 ml/24 fl oz) beef stock
1 teaspoon dried marjoram leaves
2 tablespoons Worcestershire sauce

1 Preheat the oven to moderate 180°C (350°F/Gas 4). Heat 2 tablespoons of the oil in a saucepan over medium–high heat. Cook the oxtail quickly in small batches until well browned. Place in a deep casserole dish and add the potato.

2 Heat the remaining oil in the pan. Cook the onion and carrot, stirring, over medium heat for 5 minutes. Transfer to the casserole dish. Add the mushrooms to pan and cook, stirring, for 5 minutes. Stir in flour. Reduce heat to low, and stir for 2 minutes.

3 Add the stock gradually, stirring until the liquid boils and thickens. Add the marjoram and Worcestershire sauce. Pour into the casserole dish. Bake, covered, for 1½ hours. Stir, then bake, uncovered, for a further 30 minutes.

NUTRITION PER SERVE
Protein 35 g; Fat 53 g; Carbohydrate 16 g; Dietary Fibre 3.5 g; Cholesterol 102 mg; 2825 kJ (675 cal)

Cook the oxtail pieces in small batches in the hot oil.

Cook the onion and carrot, stirring, for 5 minutes over medium heat.

Pour the sauce over the oxtail and vegetables in the casserole dish.

CHILLI CON CARNE

Preparation time: 10 minutes
Total cooking time: 50 minutes
Serves 4

1 tablespoon olive oil
1 onion, chopped
3 cloves garlic, crushed
1 stick celery, sliced
500 g (1 lb) lean beef mince
2 teaspoons chilli powder
pinch of cayenne pepper
1 tablespoon chopped oregano

400 g (13 oz) can crushed
  tomatoes
2 tablespoons tomato paste
1 teaspoon soft brown sugar
1 tablespoon cider vinegar or red
  wine vinegar
420 g (13 oz) can red kidney
  beans, drained and rinsed

1 Heat the oil in a large, heavy-based pan. Add the onion, garlic and celery and cook, stirring, over medium heat for 5 minutes, or until softened.
2 Add the mince and stir over high heat for 5 minutes, or until well browned. Add the chilli powder, cayenne and oregano. Stir well and cook over medium heat for 5 minutes.
3 Mix in the tomatoes, tomato paste and ½ cup (125 ml/4 fl oz) of water. Simmer for 30 minutes, stirring now and then.
4 Add the sugar, vinegar and beans and season to taste with salt and freshly ground black pepper. Heat through for 5 minutes before serving.

NUTRITION PER SERVE
Protein 35 g; Fat 20 g; Carbohydrate 20 g;
Dietary Fibre 10 g; Cholesterol 80 mg;
1640 kJ (390 cal)

Add the mince to the onion, garlic and celery mixture. Stir until well browned.

Add the crushed tomatoes, tomato paste and water to the mince mixture.

Stir in the sugar, vinegar and drained kidney beans and simmer for 5 minutes.

BEEF STROGANOFF

Preparation time: 25 minutes
Total cooking time: 30 minutes
Serves 6

1 kg (2 lb) piece rump steak,
   trimmed
⅓ cup (40 g/1¼ oz) plain flour
¼ teaspoon ground black pepper
¼ cup (60 ml/2 fl oz) olive oil
1 large onion, chopped
500 g (1 lb) baby mushrooms
1 tablespoon sweet paprika
1 tablespoon tomato paste
2 teaspoons French mustard
½ cup (125 ml/4 fl oz) dry white
   wine
¼ cup (60 ml/2 fl oz) chicken
   stock
¾ cup (185 g/6 oz) sour cream
1 tablespoon finely chopped fresh
   parsley

1 Slice the meat across the grain
into short, thin pieces. Combine the
flour and pepper. Toss the meat in
the seasoned flour, shaking off the
excess.
2 Heat 2 tablespoons of the oil in a
heavy-based saucepan. Cook the
meat quickly in small batches over
medium–high heat until well
browned. Drain on paper towels.
3 Heat the remaining oil in the pan.
Cook the onion over medium heat
for 3 minutes, or until soft. Add the
mushrooms and stir for 5 minutes.
4 Add the paprika, tomato paste,
mustard, wine and stock to the pan,
and bring to the boil. Reduce the
heat and simmer for 5 minutes,
uncovered, stirring occasionally.
Return the meat to the pan with the
sour cream, and stir until combined
and just heated through. Sprinkle
with the parsley just before serving.

NUTRITION PER SERVE
Protein 42 g; Fat 28 g; Carbohydrate 9.5 g;
Dietary Fibre 3.5 g; Cholesterol 147 mg;
1970 kJ (470 cal)

*Toss the meat in the seasoned flour,
shaking off any excess.*

*Cook the meat quickly in small batches
until it is well browned.*

*Add the mushrooms to the cooked onion
and stir for 5 minutes.*

*Return meat to pan with sour cream, and
stir until combined and heated through.*

BEEF AND GLOBE ARTICHOKE STEW

Preparation time: 30 minutes
Total cooking time: 2 hours 15 minutes
Serves 4–6

2 tablespoons olive oil
1 kg (2 lb) stewing beef, cut into
　　large cubes
2 red onions, sliced
4 cloves garlic, crushed
1 teaspoon cumin seeds
2 teaspoons ground cumin
1 teaspoon ground coriander
2 teaspoons sweet paprika
1 tablespoon plain flour
2 cups (500 ml/16 fl oz) beef
　　stock
1 teaspoon grated lemon rind
1 tablespoon soft brown sugar
1 tablespoon tomato paste
¼ cup (60 ml/2 fl oz) lemon juice
4 fresh globe artichokes
3 tablespoons small black olives

1 Preheat the oven to moderate 180°C (350°F/Gas 4). Heat half the oil in a large heavy-based pan. Brown the meat in batches over medium-high heat and transfer to a large casserole dish.
2 Add the remaining oil to the pan and cook the onion over medium heat for 5 minutes, or until soft. Add the garlic, cumin seeds, cumin, coriander and paprika and cook for 1 minute.
3 Add the flour, cook for 30 seconds and remove from the heat. Add the stock, return to the heat and stir until the mixture bubbles. Add to the meat with the rind, sugar and tomato paste. Cover tightly and bake for 1½ hours.
4 Meanwhile, add the lemon juice to a bowl of water. Cut the top third

from each artichoke, trim the stem to 5 cm (2 inches) and cut away the dark outer leaves. Cut the artichokes lengthways in half. Remove the prickly lavender-topped leaves in the centre and scoop out the hairy choke. Drop into the lemon-water until ready to use.
5 Drain the artichokes and add to the casserole, covering them in the liquid. Cover and cook for 30 minutes, or until tender. For a

thicker gravy, cook uncovered for 15 minutes more. Season and stir in the olives to serve.

NUTRITION PER SERVE (6)
Protein 40 g; Fat 12 g; Carbohydrate 8 g; Dietary Fibre 2 g; Cholesterol 112 mg; 1212 kJ (290 cal)

COOK'S FILE

Note: Tiny black olives have a great flavour and are sold in delicatessens.

Add the garlic and spices to the fried onion and cook for 1 minute.

Cut the trimmed artichokes lengthways in half and place them in the lemon-water.

Drain the artichokes and add them to the casserole, covering them with the liquid.

BEEF BOURGUIGNON

Preparation time: 10 minutes
Total cooking time: 2 hours
Serves 4–6

**1 kg (2 lb) topside or round steak
plain flour, seasoned with salt
    and freshly ground pepper
3 rashers bacon, rind removed
oil, for cooking
12 pickling onions
1 cup (250 ml/ 8 fl oz) red wine
2 cups (500 ml/16 fl oz) beef
    stock
1 teaspoon dried thyme**

**200 g (6½ oz) button mushrooms
2 bay leaves**

1 Trim the steak of fat and sinew and cut into 2 cm (¾ inch) cubes. Lightly toss in the seasoned flour to coat, shaking off the excess.
2 Cut the bacon into 2 cm (¾ inch) squares. Heat some oil in a large pan and quickly cook the bacon over medium heat. Remove the bacon from the pan, then add the meat and brown well in batches. Remove and set aside. Add the onions to the pan and cook until golden.
3 Return the bacon and meat to the pan with the remaining ingredients.

Bring to the boil, reduce the heat and simmer, covered, for 1½ hours, or until the meat is very tender, stirring now and then. Remove the bay leaves to serve. Mashed potato and steamed green beans are a nice accompaniment.

NUTRITION PER SERVE (6)
Protein 40 g; Fat 7 g; Carbohydrate 5 g; Dietary Fibre 1 g; Cholesterol 90 mg; 1150 kJ (275 cal)

COOK'S FILE

Storage time: Refrigerate in an airtight container for up to 3 days.

Trim the meat of fat and sinew and cut into cubes.

Fry the bacon in the hot oil over medium heat until lightly browned.

Return the bacon and meat to the pan and add the remaining ingredients.

BEEF CARBONNADE

Preparation time: 15 minutes
Total cooking time: 3 hours 25 minutes
Serves 4

1 leek, green part only
1 bay leaf
1 sprig fresh thyme
1 sprig celery leaves
4 sprigs fresh parsley
40 g (1¼ oz) butter
1 tablespoon oil
1 kg (2 lb) chuck or stewing
    steak, cubed
2 onions, sliced
2 cloves garlic, crushed
2 tablespoons plain flour
1½ cups (375 ml/12 fl oz) brown
    ale or stout
1 long bread stick
2 teaspoons French mustard
2 teaspoons butter, extra,
    softened

1 To make a bouquet garni, wrap the green part of the leek loosely around the bay leaf, thyme sprig, celery leaves and parsley, then tie together with string. Leave a long tail on the string for easy removal.

2 Preheat the oven to moderate 180°C (350°F/Gas 4). Heat the butter and oil in a large saucepan, and cook the beef in batches for 3–4 minutes, or until well browned. Remove from the pan. Reduce the heat and cook the onion and garlic for 4 minutes, or until translucent. Sprinkle in the flour, stir well, then cook for 1 minute. Combine the beer with 1½ cups (375 ml/12 fl oz) water, and pour into the pan. Stir well, scraping the pan to incorporate ingredients that are stuck to the base of the pan. Bring to the boil and return the meat to the pan. Add the bouquet garni and return to the boil. Transfer to a 2.5 litre casserole dish, cover well with foil and bake for 2½ hours.

Leave a long tail of string on the bouquet garni for easy removal.

3 Cut the bread into 2 cm (¾ inch) slices and spread with the combined mustard and extra butter. Remove the casserole from the oven, take out the bouquet garni and skim off any fat. Put the bread slices on the surface of the casserole, mustard-side up, and press down gently to cover with juice. Return to the oven and cook, uncovered, for another 30–40 minutes, or until the bread becomes crusty. Serve with steamed green vegetables.

NUTRITION PER SERVE
Protein 60 g; Fat 25 g; Carbohydrate 30 g; Dietary Fibre 3.5 g; Cholesterol 195 mg; 2455 kJ (585 cal)

Cook the beef in batches in a large saucepan until well browned all over.

BEEF AND PEPPERCORN STEW

Preparation time: 15 minutes
Total cooking time: 2 hours
Serves 4

1 kg (2 lb) chuck steak, cut into 3 cm (1¼ inch) cubes
2 teaspoons cracked black peppercorns
40 g (1¼ oz) butter
2 tablespoons oil
1 large onion, thinly sliced
2 cloves garlic, sliced
1½ tablespoons plain flour
2 tablespoons brandy

3 cups (750 ml/24 fl oz) beef stock
1 tablespoon Worcestershire sauce
2 teaspoons Dijon mustard
500 g (1 lb) baby new potatoes
¼ cup (60 ml/2 fl oz) cream
2 tablespoons chopped parsley

1 Toss the steak in the peppercorns. Heat half the butter and half the oil in a large heavy-based pan. Brown half the steak over high heat; remove and set aside. Heat the remaining butter and oil and brown the remaining steak. Remove and set aside.
2 Add the onion and garlic to the pan and cook, stirring, until the onion is golden. Add the flour and stir until browned. Remove from the heat.
3 Combine the brandy, beef stock, Worcestershire sauce and mustard, and gradually stir into the onion mixture. Return to the heat, add the steak and any juices, then simmer, covered, for 1¼ hours.
4 Add the potatoes and simmer, uncovered, for a further 30 minutes, or until the meat and potatoes are tender. Stir in the cream and parsley and season to taste with salt and freshly ground pepper.

NUTRITION PER SERVE
Protein 60 g; Fat 30 g; Carbohydrate 20 g; Dietary Fibre 3 g; Cholesterol 215 mg; 2580 kJ (615 cal)

Cut the steak into 3 cm (11/4 inch) cubes, using a sharp knife.

Add the brandy, stock, Worcestershire sauce and mustard to the onion mixture.

Add the potatoes and simmer, uncovered, for a further 30 minutes, or until tender.

BEEF IN BEER WITH CAPERS AND ANCHOVIES

Preparation time: 25 minutes
Total cooking time: 3 hours 20 minutes
Serves 4–6

1 kg (2 lb) gravy beef
plain flour, seasoned with salt
　and freshly ground pepper
olive oil, for cooking
4 cloves garlic, finely chopped
2 cups (500 ml/16 fl oz) beef
　stock
1½ cups (375 ml/12 fl oz) beer
2 onions, chopped
3 bay leaves
⅓ cup (55 g/2 oz) stuffed or

pitted green olives, sliced
6 anchovies
2 tablespoons capers, drained

1 Cut the beef into 4 cm (1½ inch) chunks, following the sinew and separation of the meat. Lightly coat in the flour. Heat 3 tablespoons of oil in a deep heavy-based pan, add the garlic, then brown the beef over high heat.
2 Add the stock, beer, onions and bay leaves, season well and bring to the boil. Reduce the heat; cover and gently simmer for 2½ hours, stirring about three times during cooking. Remove the lid and simmer for 30 minutes more. Stir, then mix in the olives.
3 Heat 2 teaspoons of oil in a small

pan. Add the anchovies and capers, gently breaking up the anchovies. Cook over medium heat for 4 minutes, or until brown and crisp. To serve, place the meat on serving plates, drizzle with the sauce, sprinkle with anchovies and capers, and season with salt and freshly cracked pepper.

NUTRITION PER SERVE (6)
Protein 40 g; Fat 6 g; Carbohydrate 4 g; Dietary Fibre 1 g; Cholesterol 115 mg; 965 kJ (230 cal)

COOK'S FILE

NOTE: The capers should be squeezed very dry before being added to the pan, or they will spit in the hot oil.

Cut the beef into large chunks, following the sinew and separation of the meat.

Add the stock, beer, onions and bay leaves to the browned beef.

Fry the anchovies and capers in a little hot oil until brown and crisp.

HOT BEEF BORSCHT

Preparation time: 30 minutes
Total cooking time: 2 hours 50 minutes
Serves 4–6

500 g (1 lb) gravy beef, cut into
    large pieces
500 g (1 lb) fresh beetroot
1 onion, finely chopped
1 carrot, cut into short strips
1 parsnip, cut into short strips
1 cup (75 g/2½ oz) finely
    shredded cabbage
sour cream and chopped fresh
    chives, to serve

1 Put the beef and 1 litre water in a large, heavy-based saucepan, and bring slowly to the boil. Reduce the heat, cover and simmer for 1 hour. Skim the surface as required.
2 Cut the stems from the beetroot, wash well and place in a large, heavy-based saucepan with 1 litre water. Bring to the boil, then reduce the heat and simmer for 40 minutes, or until tender. Drain, reserving 1 cup (250 ml/8 fl oz) of the liquid. Cool, then peel and grate the beetroot.
3 Remove the meat from the stock, cool and dice. Skim any fat from the surface of the stock. Return the meat to the stock and add the onion, carrot, parsnip, beetroot and reserved liquid. Bring to the boil, reduce the heat, cover and simmer for 45 minutes.
4 Stir in the cabbage and simmer for a further 15 minutes. Season to taste. Serve with the sour cream and chives.

NUTRITION PER SERVE (6)
Protein 20 g; Fat 10 g; Carbohydrate 10 g; Dietary Fibre 5 g; Cholesterol 80 mg; 940 kJ (225 cal)

To avoid stains, wear rubber gloves to grate the cooled beetroot.

Allow the meat to cool, then cut it into dice using a sharp knife.

Pour the reserved beetroot liquid into the soup and bring to the boil.

CHICKEN AND MUSHROOM CASSEROLE

Preparation time: 20 minutes + 5 minutes soaking
Total cooking time: 1 hour
Serves 4

20 g (¾ oz) dried porcini mushrooms
1.5 kg (3 lb) chicken pieces
¼ cup (30 g/1 oz) seasoned plain flour
2 tablespoons oil
1 large onion, chopped
2 cloves garlic, crushed
¼ cup (60 ml/2 fl oz) chicken stock
⅓ cup (80 ml/2¾ fl oz) white wine

425 g (14 oz) can peeled whole tomatoes
1 tablespoon balsamic vinegar
3 sprigs fresh thyme
1 bay leaf
300 g (10 oz) field mushrooms, thickly sliced

1 Preheat the oven to moderate 180°C (350°F/Gas 4). Put the porcini mushrooms in a bowl and cover with ¼ cup (60 ml/2 fl oz) boiling water. Leave for 5 minutes, or until the mushrooms are rehydrated.

2 Lightly toss the chicken in the seasoned flour to coat, and shake off any excess.

3 Heat the oil in a flameproof casserole dish, and cook the chicken over medium heat in batches until well browned all over. Set aside. Add the onion and garlic to the casserole, and cook for 3–5 minutes, or until onion softens. Stir in the chicken stock.

4 Return the chicken to the casserole with the porcini mushrooms (and any remaining liquid), wine, tomatoes, vinegar, thyme and bay leaf. Cover and bake for 30 minutes.

5 After 30 minutes, remove the lid and add the field mushrooms. Return to the oven and cook, uncovered, for 15–20 minutes, or until the sauce thickens slightly. Serve immediately.

NUTRITION PER SERVE
Protein 55 g; Fat 10 g; Carbohydrate 7 g; Dietary Fibre 4 g; Cholesterol 115 mg; 1515 kJ (360 cal)

Cover the porcini mushrooms with boiling water and soak until rehydrated.

Lightly toss the chicken pieces in the flour and shake off any excess.

Add the chicken to the casserole and cook in batches until brown.

CREAMY TOMATO AND CHICKEN STEW

Preparation time: 35 minutes
Total cooking time: 50 minutes
Serves 4–6

4 rashers bacon
2 tablespoons oil
50 g (1¾ oz) butter
300 g (10 oz) small button
    mushrooms, halved
1.5 kg (3 lb) chicken pieces
2 onions, chopped
2 cloves garlic, crushed
400 g (13 oz) can tomatoes
1 cup (250 ml/8 fl oz) chicken
    stock
1 cup (250 ml/8 fl oz) cream
2 tablespoons chopped parsley
2 tablespoons lemon thyme
    leaves

1 Chop the bacon into large pieces. Place a large, heavy-based pan over medium heat. Brown the bacon, then remove and set aside on paper towels.

2 Heat half the oil and a third of the butter in the pan until foaming, then stir in the mushrooms and cook until softened and golden brown. Remove from the pan with a slotted spoon.

3 Add the remaining oil to the pan with a little more butter. When the oil is hot, brown the chicken pieces in batches over high heat until the skin is golden all over and a little crisp. Remove from the pan.

4 Heat the remaining butter in the pan. Add the onion and garlic and cook over medium-high heat for about 3 minutes, or until softened. Pour in the tomatoes, stock and cream. Return the bacon, mushrooms

and chicken pieces to the pan and simmer over medium-low heat for 25 minutes. Stir in the herbs, season with salt and freshly ground pepper and simmer for another 5 minutes before serving.

NUTRITION PER SERVE (6)
Protein 70 g; Fat 40 g; Carbohydrate 7 g; Dietary Fibre 3 g; Cholesterol 215 mg; 2650 kJ (630 cal)

When the oil and butter are foaming, add the mushrooms and cook until soft.

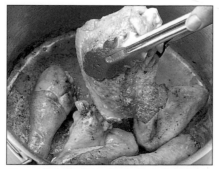

Brown the chicken pieces in batches over high heat until the skin is golden and crisp.

Add the tomatoes, stock and cream to the softened onion and garlic.

BRAISED CHICKEN WITH CHICKPEAS

Preparation time: 35 minutes
Total cooking time: 1 hour 35 minutes
Serves 4

50 g (1¾ oz) butter
1 onion, roughly chopped
3 cloves garlic, crushed
1 carrot, finely chopped
½ celery stick, finely chopped
1.5 kg (3 lb) chicken pieces
    (about 8 portions)
⅓ cup (80 ml/2¾ fl oz) Marsala
1 cup (250 ml/8 fl oz) chicken
    stock
2 tablespoons lemon juice
½ cup (40 g/1¼ oz) fresh
    breadcrumbs

300 g (10 oz) can chickpeas,
    rinsed and drained
200 g (6½ oz) button mushrooms,
    sliced
2 tablespoons shredded fresh
    mint
2 tablespoons chopped fresh
    parsley

1 Heat half the butter in a large, heavy-based pan and cook the onion over medium heat until soft. Add the garlic, carrot and celery and cook over gentle heat for 5 minutes. Remove from the pan and set aside.
2 Melt the remaining butter in the pan and brown the chicken in batches over high heat. Return all the chicken to the pan with the carrot and celery mixture. Quickly add the Marsala and stir well, scraping the sides and base of the pan. Add the stock and lemon juice, and bring to the boil. Reduce the heat and simmer gently for 1 hour, stirring occasionally.
3 Remove the chicken; keep warm. In a food processor, purée the contents of the pan, then add the breadcrumbs and blend for another 15 seconds.
4 Return the chicken to the pan, pour in the purée, add the chickpeas and mushrooms and simmer, covered, for 15 minutes. Season to taste, and scatter with mint and parsley to serve.

NUTRITION PER SERVE
Protein 120 g; Fat 30 g; Carbohydrate 50 g; Dietary Fibre 15 g; Cholesterol 260 mg; 3900 kJ (930 cal)

Gently fry the garlic, carrot and celery in the butter for 5 minutes.

Pour the Marsala over the vegetables and chicken, stirring well.

Add the fresh breadcrumbs to the puréed vegetable mixture and process until smooth.

GREEN CHICKEN CURRY

Preparation time: 40 minutes
Total cooking time: 30 minutes
Serves 4–6

2 cups (500 ml/16 fl oz) coconut
   cream (do not shake the can)
4 tablespoons green curry paste
2 tablespoons grated palm sugar
   or soft brown sugar
2 tablespoons fish sauce
4 kaffir lime leaves, finely
   shredded
1 kg (2 lb) chicken thigh or
   breast fillets, cut into thick
   strips
200 g (6½ oz) bamboo shoots, cut
   into thick strips
100 g (3½ oz) snake beans, cut
   into 5 cm (2 inch) lengths
½ cup (15 g/½ oz) fresh Thai
   basil leaves

1 Place ½ cup (125 ml/4 fl oz) of the
thick coconut cream from the top of

the can in a wok, and bring to the
boil. Add the curry paste, then
reduce the heat and simmer for 15
minutes, or until fragrant and the oil
starts to separate from the cream.
Add the palm sugar, fish sauce and
kaffir lime leaves to the pan.
2 Stir in the remaining coconut
cream and the chicken, bamboo
shoots and beans, and simmer for 15
minutes, or until the chicken is
tender. Stir in the Thai basil and
serve with rice.

*Lift off the thick cream from the top of the
can of coconut cream.*

NUTRITION PER SERVE (6)
Protein 40 g; Fat 22 g; Carbohydrate 11 g;
Dietary Fibre 2 g; Cholesterol 85 mg;
1698 kJ (405 cal)

NOTE: Do not shake the can of
coconut cream because good-quality
coconut cream has a layer of very
thick cream at the top that has
separated from the rest of the cream.
This has a higher fat content, which
causes it to split or separate more
readily than the rest of the coconut
cream or milk.

*Simmer the coconut cream and curry
paste until the oil separates.*

CHICKEN MARSALA

Preparation time: 20 minutes
Total cooking time: 1 hour 10 minutes
Serves 4

¼ cup (60 ml/2 fl oz) olive oil
3 leeks, finely sliced
1 teaspoon finely chopped
   rosemary
3 bay leaves, torn
1 kg (2 lb) chicken pieces
plain flour, seasoned with salt
   and freshly ground pepper
1 large eggplant, cut into cubes
2 zucchini, roughly chopped
½ cup (125 ml/4 fl oz) Marsala
300 ml (10 fl oz) chicken stock
2 cups (500 ml/16 fl oz) tomato
   purée

200 g (6½ oz) button mushrooms,
   halved

1 Heat the oil in a large, heavy-based pan. Fry the leek, rosemary and bay leaves over low heat for 5 minutes, or until soft, stirring occasionally. Remove with a slotted spoon, leaving as much oil in the pan as possible.
2 Toss the chicken pieces in the seasoned flour. Add the chicken to the pan and brown well in batches over medium heat. Return all the chicken to the pan with the leek mixture.
3 Add the eggplant and zucchini and cook, stirring, for 2–3 minutes, or until softened, turning the chicken pieces over. Add the Marsala and stock and cook for about 15 minutes over medium-high heat.

4 Add the tomato purée and season well with salt and pepper. Bring to the boil, turning the chicken pieces in the sauce. Reduce the heat to a very gentle simmer, then cover and cook for 35 minutes. Add the mushrooms and cook, uncovered, for 5 minutes.

NUTRITION PER SERVE
Protein 63 g; Fat 20 g; Carbohydrate 13 g; Dietary Fibre 9 g; Cholesterol 125 mg; 2200 kJ (530 cal)

COOK'S FILE

Note: Marsala is a famous Italian fortified wine. It has a smoky, rich flavour and ranges from dry to sweet.

Remove the softened leeks and herbs from the pan with a slotted spoon.

Add the chopped eggplant and zucchini to the chicken and leek mixture.

Stir in the tomato purée and season well with salt and pepper.

CHICKEN CALVADOS WITH GLAZED APPLES

Preparation time: 15 minutes
Total cooking time: 1 hour 10 minutes
Serves 4

1.25 kg (2 lb 8 oz) chicken pieces
plain flour, seasoned with salt
    and freshly ground pepper
2 tablespoons light olive oil
30 g (1 oz) butter
1 large onion, roughly chopped
1 tablespoon chopped marjoram
1 chicken stock cube, crumbled
¾ cup (185 ml/6 fl oz) apple juice
⅓ cup (80 ml/2¾ fl oz) Calvados
¾ cup (185 ml/6 fl oz) cream

Glazed Apples
2 red apples
40 g (1¼ oz) butter
2 teaspoons sugar

1 Preheat the oven to moderate 180°C (350°F/Gas 4). Trim the chicken of excess fat and sinew, then toss in the flour to coat, shaking off any excess. In a large, heavy-based pan, heat the oil and butter and brown the chicken all over, in batches if necessary. Transfer to a large casserole dish.
2 Add the onion to the pan and cook over low heat until soft but not brown. Add the marjoram, stock cube, apple juice and Calvados and bring to the boil, stirring. Season well and simmer for 5 minutes.
3 Pour the sauce over the chicken and bake, covered, for 45 minutes or until the chicken is tender. Stir in the cream and bake for 5 minutes—the sauce will be thin but delicious.
4 Meanwhile, core (but do not peel) the apples, then cut into wedges. Melt the butter in a pan, add the apples and sugar and cook over very low heat, turning occasionally, until tender and glazed. Serve with the casserole.

NUTRITION PER SERVE
Protein 70 g; Fat 50 g; Carbohydrate 20 g; Dietary Fibre 2 g; Cholesterol 265 mg; 3615 kJ (860 cal)

Toss the trimmed chicken lightly in the flour to coat, shaking off any excess.

Add the marjoram, stock cube, apple juice and Calvados to the fried onions.

Glaze the apple wedges in the sugar and butter and cook on both sides until tender.

41

CHICKEN CHASSEUR

Preparation time: 20 minutes
Total cooking time: 1 hour 30 minutes
Serves 4

1 kg (2 lb) chicken thigh fillets
2 tablespoons oil
1 clove garlic, crushed
1 large onion, sliced
100 g (3¼ oz) button mushrooms, sliced
1 teaspoon thyme leaves
400 g (13 oz) can chopped tomatoes

¼ cup (60 ml/2 fl oz) chicken stock
¼ cup (60 ml/2 fl oz) white wine
1 tablespoon tomato paste

1 Preheat the oven to moderate 180°C (350°F/Gas 4). Trim the chicken of excess fat and sinew. Heat the oil in a heavy-based frying pan and brown the chicken in batches over medium heat. Drain on paper towels, then transfer to a casserole dish.
2 Add the garlic, onion and mushrooms to the pan and cook over medium heat for 5 minutes, or until

soft. Add to the chicken with the thyme and tomatoes.
3 Combine the stock, wine and tomato paste and pour over the chicken. Cover and bake for 1¼ hours, or until the chicken is tender.

NUTRITION PER SERVE
Protein 60 g; Fat 15 g; Carbohydrate 6 g; Dietary Fibre 2 g; Cholesterol 125 mg; 1710 kJ (410 cal)

COOK'S FILE

Storage time: This dish may be cooked a day ahead. Refrigerate in an airtight container overnight.

Brown the chicken in the hot oil over medium heat and drain on paper towels.

Add the garlic, onion and mushrooms to the pan and cook until soft.

Pour the combined stock, wine and tomato paste over the chicken mixture.

CHICKEN WITH SHERRY, RAISINS AND PINE NUTS

Preparation time: 30 minutes
Total cooking time: 50 minutes
Serves 4

1.5 kg (3 lb) chicken pieces (about 8 portions)
plain flour, seasoned with salt and freshly ground pepper
¼ cup (60 ml/2 fl oz) olive oil
2 onions, thinly sliced
2 red capsicums, sliced
4 cloves garlic, finely sliced
1 cup (250 ml/8 fl oz) chicken stock
½ cup (125 ml/4 fl oz) dry sherry
½ cup (125 ml/4 fl oz) orange juice
125 g (4 oz) raisins
125 g (4 oz) pine nuts, toasted

1 Toss the chicken in the seasoned flour to coat. Heat the oil in a large, heavy-based pan. Brown the chicken in batches over medium heat until crisp and golden all over. Remove from the pan and set aside.

2 Drain the pan of excess oil and add the onion, capsicum and garlic. Cover the pan tightly and cook for about 3 minutes.

3 Add the chicken, chicken stock, sherry, orange juice and raisins and season to taste with salt and freshly ground pepper. Cover and simmer for about 35 minutes, turning the chicken now and then in the sauce.

4 Remove the chicken, keep warm and simmer sauce for 5 minutes to thicken. Pour sauce over the chicken and scatter with pine nuts to serve.

NUTRITION PER SERVE
Protein 93 g; Fat 45 g; Carbohydrate 35 g; Dietary Fibre 6 g; Cholesterol 190 mg; 3980 kJ (950 cal).

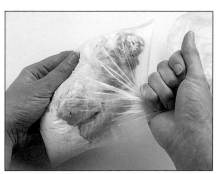

Toss the chicken in the seasoned flour to coat evenly all over.

Add the onion, capsicum and garlic to the pan. Cover and cook for 3 minutes.

Add the chicken, stock, sherry, orange juice and raisins to the capsicum mixture.

CHICKEN AND ORANGE CASSEROLE

Preparation time: 50 minutes
Total cooking time: 1 hour 30 minutes
Serves 4–6

2 small chickens
1 tablespoon olive oil
2 thick slices bacon, rind
    removed and thinly sliced
50 g (1¾ oz) butter
16 small pickling onions, peeled,
    ends left intact
2–3 cloves garlic, crushed
3 teaspoons grated fresh ginger
2 teaspoons grated orange rind
2 teaspoons ground cumin
2 teaspoons ground coriander
2 tablespoons honey
1 cup (250 ml/8 fl oz) fresh
    orange juice
1 cup (250 ml/8 fl oz) white wine
½ cup (125 ml/4 fl oz) chicken or
    vegetable stock
1 bunch baby carrots
1 large parsnip, peeled
fresh coriander and orange zest,
    to serve

1 Using a sharp knife or a pair of kitchen scissors, cut each chicken into 8 pieces, discarding the backbone. Remove any excess fat and discard (remove the skin as well, if preferred).
2 Heat about a teaspoon of the oil in a large, deep, heavy-based pan. Add the bacon and cook over medium heat for 2–3 minutes or until just crisp. Remove from the pan and set aside to drain on paper towels. Add the remaining oil and half the butter to the pan. Cook the onions over medium heat until dark golden brown. Shake the pan occasionally to ensure even cooking and browning. Remove from the pan and set aside.
3 Add the chicken pieces to the pan and brown in small batches over medium heat. Remove from the pan and drain on paper towels.
4 Add the remaining butter to the pan. Stir in the garlic, ginger, orange rind, cumin, coriander and honey, and cook, stirring, for 1 minute. Add the orange juice, wine and stock to the pan. Bring to the boil, then reduce the heat and simmer for 1 minute.

Return the chicken pieces to the pan, cover and leave to simmer over low heat for 40 minutes.
5 Return the onions and bacon to the pan and simmer, covered, for a further 15 minutes. Remove the lid and leave to simmer for a further 15 minutes.
6 Trim the carrots, leaving a little green stalk, and wash well or peel if necessary. Cut the parsnip into small batons. Add the carrots and parsnip to the pan. Cover and cook for 5–10 minutes, or until the carrots and parsnip are just tender. Do not overcook the carrots or they will lose their bright colouring. When

you are ready to serve, arrange 2–3 chicken pieces on each plate. Arrange a couple of carrots and a few parsnip batons with the chicken and spoon a little sauce over the top. Garnish with the coriander leaves and orange zest.

NUTRITION PER SERVE
Protein 42 g; Fat 12 g; Carbohydrate 22 g;
Dietary Fibre 2 g; Cholesterol 135 mg;
1635 kJ (395 cal)

Cut each chicken into 8 pieces using a knife or pair of scissors.

Cook the pickling onions in the oil and butter until they are dark golden brown.

Brown the chicken pieces in batches and drain on paper towels.

Add the orange juice, white wine and stock to the pan, and bring to the boil.

Return the browned pickling onions and cooked bacon to the pan.

Cut the parsnip into batons and leave the stalks on the carrots to provide colour.

COQ AU VIN

Preparation time: 20 minutes
Total cooking time: 1 hour
Serves 6

2 sprigs of thyme
4 sprigs of parsley
2 bay leaves
2 kg (4 lb) chicken pieces
plain flour, seasoned with salt
    and freshly ground pepper
¼ cup (60 ml/2 fl oz) oil
4 thick bacon rashers, sliced
12 pickling onions
2 cloves garlic, crushed
2 tablespoons brandy

1½ cups (375 ml/12 fl oz) red
    wine
1½ cups (375 ml/12 fl oz) chicken
    stock
¼ cup (60 g/2 oz) tomato paste
250 g (8 oz) button mushrooms
fresh herbs, for sprinkling

1 To make the bouquet garni, wrap the thyme, parsley and bay leaves in a small square of muslin and tie well with string, or tie them between two 5 cm (2 inch) lengths of celery.
2 Toss the chicken in flour to coat, shaking off any excess. In a heavy-based pan, heat 2 tablespoons of oil and brown the chicken in batches over medium heat. Drain on paper towels.

3 Wipe the pan clean with paper towels and heat the remaining oil. Add the bacon, onions and garlic and cook, stirring, until the onions are browned. Add the chicken, brandy, wine, stock, bouquet garni and tomato paste. Bring to the boil, reduce the heat and simmer, covered, for 30 minutes.
4 Stir in the mushrooms and simmer, uncovered, for 10 minutes, or until the chicken is tender and the sauce has thickened. Remove the bouquet garni, sprinkle with fresh herbs and serve with crusty French bread.

NUTRITION PER SERVE
Protein 80 g; Fat 20 g; Carbohydrate 7 g;
Dietary Fibre 2 g; Cholesterol 180 mg;
2420 kJ (580 cal)

Wrap the thyme, parsley and bay leaves in a small square of muslin.

In batches, brown the chicken in the hot oil over medium heat.

Return the chicken to the pan with the liquids, bouquet garni and tomato paste.

CHICKEN CACCIATORE

Preparation time: 20 minutes
Total cooking time: 1 hour 15 minutes
Serves 4

1.25 kg (2 lb 8 oz) chicken pieces
2 tablespoons plain flour
1 tablespoon olive oil
1 large onion, finely chopped
2 cloves garlic, chopped
2 x 425 g (14 oz) cans tomatoes,
   roughly chopped

2 cups (500 ml/16 fl oz) chicken
   stock
½ cup (125 ml/4 fl oz) white wine
2 tablespoons tomato paste
1 teaspoon caster sugar
2 tablespoons chopped basil
2 tablespoons chopped parsley
½ cup (90 g/3 oz) black olives

1 Toss the chicken in the flour to coat. Heat the oil in a large, heavy-based pan and brown the chicken in batches over medium heat. Remove from the pan and drain on paper towels.

2 Cook the onion and garlic in the pan for 10 minutes over low heat, stirring. Add tomatoes, stock and wine. Bring to the boil, reduce the heat and simmer for 15 minutes. Add tomato paste, sugar and chicken; mix well.
3 Cover and simmer for 30 minutes, then add the herbs and olives and season to taste. Simmer for another 15 minutes, stirring occasionally.

NUTRITION PER SERVE
Protein 60 g; Fat 10 g; Carbohydrate 15 g; Dietary Fibre 4 g; Cholesterol 125 mg; 1800 kJ (480 cal).

Brown the chicken in batches in the hot oil and drain on paper towels.

Add the tomatoes, stock and wine to the softened onion and garlic mixture.

Stir in the herbs, olives and salt and pepper to taste.

CHICKEN WITH CREAMY CURRY SAUCE

Preparation time: 25 minutes
Total cooking time: 40 minutes
Serves 4

1 tablespoon oil
50 g (1¾ oz) butter
1 onion, chopped
2 cloves garlic, crushed
2 teaspoons grated fresh ginger
1 green chilli, seeded and finely
    chopped
¼ teaspoon crushed cardamom
    seeds
1 teaspoon garam masala
1 teaspoon ground turmeric

1 tablespoon plain flour
1½ cups (375 ml/12 fl oz) chicken
    stock
⅓ cup (80 ml/2¾ fl oz) brandy
½ cup (125 ml/4 fl oz) cream
4 large chicken breast fillets,
    each cut into thirds and
    flattened with a meat mallet
flaked toasted almonds, to serve
chopped fresh coriander, to serve

1 Heat the oil and half the butter in a large, deep frying pan. Add the onion and cook over medium heat until soft and transparent. Add the garlic, ginger and chilli and cook for 1 minute. Add the cardamom, garam masala and turmeric and cook for 1 minute. Stir in the flour and cook for 1 minute.

2 Remove from the heat. Gradually mix in the combined chicken stock, brandy and cream, stirring constantly. Return to the heat. Cook, stirring, until the sauce boils and thickens. Cover and simmer over low heat for 15 minutes.

3 Meanwhile, heat the remaining butter in a frying pan and brown the chicken pieces. Add the chicken to the sauce and cook for a further 10–15 minutes to reduce. Season with salt and black pepper. Serve scattered with toasted almonds and coriander.

NUTRITION PER SERVE
Protein 40 g; Fat 35 g; Carbohydrate 5 g; Dietary Fibre 2 g; Cholesterol 155 mg; 2295 kJ (545 cal)

Seed and finely chop the green chilli with a sharp knife.

Cook the onion over medium heat until it turns soft and transparent.

Gradually add the combined stock, brandy and cream, stirring constantly.

MEDITERRANEAN CHICKEN

Preparation time: 30 minutes
Total cooking time: 1 hour 10 minutes
Serves 4

8 chicken thigh cutlets
2 tablespoons olive oil
150 g (5 oz) French shallots
4 cloves garlic
½ cup (125 ml/4 fl oz) white wine
425 g (14 oz) can chopped
    tomatoes
12 Kalamata olives
1 tablespoon red wine vinegar
2 teaspoons tomato paste
1 tablespoon oregano leaves
1 tablespoon chopped basil leaves
1 teaspoon sugar
4 slices prosciutto
1 teaspoon grated lemon rind
½ cup (30 g/1 oz) chopped
    parsley
1 tablespoon capers, rinsed

1 Preheat the oven to moderate 180°C (350°C/Gas 4). Remove the skin and fat from the chicken thighs. Heat half the oil in a large pan and brown the chicken over high heat for 3–4 minutes on each side, then arrange in a large flameproof casserole dish.

2 Heat the remaining oil in the same pan. Add the shallots and garlic and cook over medium heat for 4 minutes, or until soft but not brown. Add the wine and bring to the boil.

3 Add the tomatoes, olives, vinegar, tomato paste, herbs and sugar. Season with salt and cracked black pepper. Boil, stirring, for 2 minutes, then pour over the chicken and cover with a tight-fitting lid. Bake for 45 minutes, or until the chicken is tender.

4 Meanwhile, place the prosciutto slices in a single layer in a frying pan, without any oil. Dry fry for 3 minutes, or until crispy, turning once. Break into large chunks and set aside.

5 Arrange the chicken on a serving dish; cover and keep warm. Transfer the casserole to the stove top and boil the pan juices for 5 minutes, or until thickened, stirring occasionally. Spoon the juices over the chicken, sprinkle with lemon rind, parsley and capers and top with the prosciutto to serve.

NUTRITION PER SERVE
Protein 75 g; Fat 25 g; Carbohydrate 15 g; Dietary Fibre 8 g; Cholesterol 155 mg; 2390 kJ (570 cal)

When the shallots and garlic are soft, add the wine.

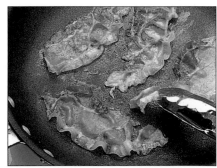

Place the prosciutto slices in a single layer in a dry frying pan and fry until crisp.

49

COUNTRY-STYLE CHICKEN WITH BABY VEGETABLES

Preparation time: 45 minutes
Total cooking time: 2 hours
Serves 4

1.5 kg (3 lb) chicken pieces
   (about 8 portions)
60 g (2 oz) clarified butter
12 baby pickling onions
1 cup (250 ml/8 fl oz) dry white
   wine
1 cup (250 ml/8 fl oz) chicken
   stock
1 cup (250 ml/8 fl oz) cream
12 baby carrots
16 snowpeas
16 asparagus spears
12 button mushrooms
1 tablespoon chopped chives

1 Season the chicken portions with a little salt and pepper. Heat half the butter in a frying pan, then brown the chicken in batches for 2–3 minutes on each side to seal the flavours. Place in a casserole dish and add the onions. Preheat the oven to moderately hot 200°C (400°F/Gas 6).
2 Pour the wine into the frying pan and stir over medium heat, scraping down the side and base of the pan. Add the stock and whisk in the cream. Bring to the boil, then reduce the heat and simmer for 20 minutes. Pour the sauce over the chicken; cover and bake for 1 hour 10 minutes.
3 Meanwhile, bring a pan of salted water to the boil. In separate batches, boil or steam the carrots, snowpeas and asparagus until just cooked, but still slightly crunchy. Plunge in iced water, then drain and set aside.
4 Heat the remaining butter in a

frying pan. Sauté the mushrooms for 2–3 minutes, stirring constantly.
5 Place the mushrooms on top of the stew with the blanched vegetables and cook for another 20 minutes, or until the chicken is tender. Skim off any fat, stir carefully to mix all the

vegetables through and sprinkle with the chives to serve.

NUTRITION PER SERVE
Protein 95 g; Fat 50 g; Carbohydrate 15 g; Dietary Fibre 4 g; Cholesterol 350 mg; 4040 kJ (965 cal)

Lightly brown the seasoned chicken in half the melted butter.

Plunge the blanched vegetables into a bowl of iced water to stop them cooking.

Place the drained blanched vegetables on top of the stew and cook for 20 minutes.

Peel two strips of orange rind. Remove the pith and slice the orange into rounds.

Combine the chicken stock and wine and add to the softened onion mixture.

Grill the capsicum, skin-side-up, until the skin is blistered and black.

Stir the capsicum strips, orange slices, olives and parsley into the sauce.

MAJORCAN CHICKEN

Preparation time: 30 minutes
Total cooking time: 1 hour 30 minutes
Serves 4

2 tablespoons olive oil
30 g (1 oz) butter
1.5 kg (3 lb) chicken pieces
1 orange
1 red onion, thinly sliced
2 cloves garlic, chopped
¾ cup (185 ml/6 fl oz) chicken
    stock
½ cup (125 ml/4 fl oz) white wine
1 tablespoon plain flour
1 red capsicum, quartered
12 stuffed green olives
3 tablespoons chopped parsley

1 Preheat the oven to moderate 180°C (350°F/Gas 4). Heat the oil and butter in a large pan. Brown the chicken in batches over high heat and transfer to a flameproof casserole dish.
2 Cut two large strips of rind from the orange and set aside. Remove the pith from the orange, then slice the orange into thin rounds. Set aside.
3 Cook the onion and garlic in the pan for 3 minutes over medium heat, or until softened. Combine the stock and wine. Stir the flour into the pan, then slowly add the stock and wine and stir until the mixture comes to the boil. Add the orange rind strips, then pour over the chicken. Cover and bake for 1 hour.
4 Meanwhile, grill the capsicum, skin-side-up, for 8 minutes, or until black and blistered. Place in a plastic bag, seal and allow to cool. Peel away the skin and cut the flesh into strips.
5 Remove the chicken from the dish; cover and keep warm. Bring the sauce to the boil on the stove top, skimming off the fat. Boil for 5 minutes to thicken slightly. Add the capsicum strips, orange slices, olives and parsley. To serve, remove the orange rind, season to taste and spoon the sauce over the chicken.

NUTRITION PER SERVE
Protein 90 g; Fat 25 g; Carbohydrate 10 g; Dietary Fibre 4 g; Cholesterol 205 mg; 2700 kJ (645 cal)

CHICKEN, LEEK AND SWEET POTATO ONE-POT

Preparation time: 15 minutes
Total cooking time: 1 hour 40 minutes
Serves 4

600 g (1¼ lb) orange sweet
   potato
2 tablespoons olive oil
1.5 kg (3 lb) chicken pieces
1 leek, cut into 2 cm (¾ inch)
   slices
2 cloves garlic, crushed
2 tablespoons plain flour
2 cups (500 ml/16 fl oz) chicken
   stock
2 tablespoons fresh thyme

1 Preheat the oven to hot 220°C (425°F/Gas 7). Peel the sweet potato and cut it into chunks. Heat 1 tablespoon of the oil in a large flameproof casserole dish. Cook the chicken in batches for 3–4 minutes, or until browned. Set aside. Add the remaining oil and cook the leek and garlic for 2 minutes, or until soft.
2 Add the flour to the dish and cook, stirring, for about 1 minute to brown the flour. Gradually add the stock, stirring until the sauce boils and thickens. Remove from the heat. Return the chicken to the pan.
3 Add the sweet potato and half the thyme. Bake, covered, for 1½ hours, or until chicken is cooked through and sweet potato is tender. Season, and scatter with the remaining thyme. Serve with steamed rice.

NUTRITION PER SERVE
Protein 80 g; Fat 25 g; Carbohydrate 25 g; Dietary Fibre 4 g; Cholesterol 260 mg; 2778 kJ (665 cal)

Brown the chicken pieces, in batches, until they are browned all over.

Gradually add stock to flour mixture, then stir until the sauce boils and thickens.

Add the sweet potato pieces to the casserole dish, along with half the thyme.

APRICOT CHICKEN

Preparation time: 10 minutes
Total cooking time: 1 hour
Serves 6

**6 chicken thigh cutlets, skin
removed**
**425 ml (14 fl oz) can apricot
nectar**
**40 g (1¼ oz) packet French onion
soup mix**
**425 g (14 oz) can apricot halves
in natural juice, drained**
¼ cup (60 g/2 oz) sour cream

1 Preheat the oven to moderate
180°C (350°F/Gas 4). Put the chicken
thigh cutlets in a casserole dish. Mix
the apricot nectar with the French
onion soup mix until well combined,
and pour over the chicken.
2 Bake, covered, for 50 minutes,
then add the apricot halves and bake
for a further 5 minutes. Stir in the
sour cream just before serving.
Delicious served with creamy
mashed potato or rice to soak up the
juices.

*Pour in the apricot nectar and stir to
combine with the soup mix.*

NUTRITION PER SERVE
Protein 23 g; Fat 6 g; Carbohydrate 10 g;
Dietary Fibre 0 g; Cholesterol 63 mg; 780
kJ (187 cal)

NOTE: You can use low-fat sour
cream in this recipe if you prefer.

*Add the apricot halves to the chicken and
bake for 5 minutes more.*

MULLIGATAWNY

Preparation time: 20 minutes
Total cooking time: 1 hour 15 minutes
Serves 4

30 g (1 oz) butter
375 g (12 oz) chicken thigh
   cutlets, skin and fat removed
1 large onion, finely chopped
1 apple, peeled, cored and diced
1 tablespoon curry paste
2 tablespoons plain flour
¼ cup (50 g/1¾ oz) basmati rice

3 cups (750 ml/24 fl oz) chicken
   stock
1 tablespoon chutney
1 tablespoon lemon juice
¼ cup (60 ml/2 fl oz) cream

1 Heat the butter in a large heavy-based saucepan. Cook the chicken for 5 minutes, or until browned, then remove and set aside. Add the onion, apple and curry paste to the pan. Cook for 5 minutes, or until the onion is soft. Stir in the flour and cook for 2 minutes, then add half the stock. Stir until the mixture boils and thickens.

2 Return the chicken to the pan with the remaining stock. Stir until boiling, then reduce the heat, cover and simmer for 1 hour. Add the rice for the last 15 minutes of cooking.

3 Remove the chicken from the pan. Remove the meat from the bones, dice finely and return to the pan. Add the chutney, lemon juice and cream, and season to taste.

NUTRITION PER SERVE
Protein 25 g; Fat 16 g; Carbohydrate 25 g;
Dietary Fibre 2 g; Cholesterol 28 mg;
1396 kJ (333 cal)

Once the mixture has thickened, return the browned chicken thighs to the pan.

Add the basmati rice to the soup during the last 15 minutes of cooking.

Add the chutney, lemon juice and cream at the end of cooking.

CANJA (PORTUGUESE CHICKEN BROTH WITH RICE)

Preparation time: 15 minutes
Total cooking time: 1 hour
Serves 6

2.5 litres chicken stock
1 onion, cut into thin wedges
1 teaspoon grated lemon rind
1 sprig fresh mint
500 g (1 lb) potatoes, chopped
1 tablespoon olive oil
2 chicken breast fillets
1 cup (200 g/6½ oz) long-grain rice
2 tablespoons lemon juice
fresh shredded mint, to garnish

1 Combine the chicken stock, onion, lemon rind, mint sprig, potato and olive oil in a large saucepan. Slowly bring to the boil, then reduce the heat, add the chicken breasts and simmer gently for 20–25 minutes, or until the chicken is cooked through.
2 Remove the chicken breasts and discard the mint sprig. Cool the chicken, then cut it into thin slices.
3 Meanwhile, add the rice to the pan and simmer for 25–30 minutes, or until the rice is tender. Return the sliced chicken to the pan, add the lemon juice and stir for 1–2 minutes, or until the chicken is warmed through. Season, and serve garnished with mint.

NUTRITION PER SERVE
Protein 20 g; Fat 5 g; Carbohydrate 38 g; Dietary Fibre 2 g; Cholesterol 37 mg; 1197 kJ (286 cal)

Simmer the chicken for 20–25 minutes, or until cooked through.

Once the cooked chicken has cooled, cut it into thin slices.

Add the rice to the pan and simmer until the rice is tender.

CREAMY CHICKEN WITH MUSHROOMS

Preparation time: 20 minutes
Total cooking time: 40 minutes
Serves 6

2 tablespoons olive oil
200 g (6½ oz) button mushrooms, halved
200 g (6½ oz) field mushrooms, chopped
1 small red capsicum, sliced
4 chicken breast fillets, cut into bite-sized pieces
2 tablespoons plain flour
1 cup (250 ml/8 fl oz) chicken stock

½ cup (125 ml/4 fl oz) red wine
3 spring onions, finely chopped
1¼ cups (315 ml/10 fl oz) cream
1 tablespoon chopped fresh chives
1 tablespoon finely chopped fresh parsley
¼ teaspoon turmeric

1 Heat the oil in a large heavy-based pan and add the button and field mushrooms and capsicum. Cook over medium heat for 4 minutes, or until soft. Remove and set aside.
2 Add the chicken to the pan in batches and brown quickly over medium-high heat. Sprinkle with the flour and cook for a further 2 minutes, or until the flour is golden.

Add the stock and wine and bring to the boil. Cover and simmer for 10 minutes, or until the chicken is tender.
3 Add the spring onion and cream, return to the boil and simmer for 10–15 minutes, or until the cream has reduced and thickened. Return the mushrooms and capsicum to the pan and add the chives, parsley and turmeric. Stir, season to taste and simmer for a further 5 minutes to heat through.

NUTRITION PER SERVE
Protein 40 g; Fat 33 g; Carbohydrate 6.5 g; Dietary Fibre 2 g; Cholesterol 150 mg; 2060 kJ (493 cal)

Choose large field mushrooms and wipe them with a damp cloth before chopping.

Add the spring onion and cream to the pan and return to the boil.

Add the mushrooms, capsicum, chives, parsley and turmeric.

PERSIAN CHICKEN

Preparation time: 20 minutes
Total cooking time: 1 hour
Serves 6

1.5 kg (3 lb) small chicken thighs
½ cup (60 g/2 oz) plain flour
2 tablespoons olive oil
1 large onion, chopped
2 cloves garlic, chopped
½ teaspoon ground cinnamon
4 ripe tomatoes, chopped
6 fresh dates, stones removed, halved
2 tablespoons currants

2 cups (500 ml/16 fl oz) rich chicken stock
2 teaspoons finely grated lemon rind
½ cup (80 g/2¾ oz) almonds, toasted and roughly chopped
2 tablespoons chopped fresh parsley

1 Coat the chicken pieces with flour and shake off any excess. Heat the oil in a large heavy-based pan over medium heat. Brown the chicken on all sides, turning regularly, and then remove from the pan. Drain any excess oil from the pan.
2 Add the onion, garlic and ground cinnamon to the pan and cook, stirring regularly, for 5 minutes, or until the onion is soft.
3 Add the tomato, dates, currants and stock, and bring to the boil. Return the chicken to the pan, cover with the sauce, reduce the heat and simmer, uncovered, for 30 minutes. Add the lemon rind and season to taste. Bring back to the boil and boil for 5 minutes, or until thickened. Sprinkle with the almonds and parsley, and serve with buttered rice.

NUTRITION PER SERVE
Protein 42 g; Fat 16 g; Carbohydrate 17 g; Dietary Fibre 3.5 g; Cholesterol 83 mg; 1597 kJ (382 cal)

Coat the chicken pieces with the flour and shake off any excess.

Brown the chicken on all sides, turning regularly to prevent it from sticking.

Add the tomato, dates, currants and stock to the softened onion.

TURKEY OSSO BUCO

Preparation time: 25 minutes +
  thawing
Total cooking time: 1 hour 30 minutes
Serves 4–6

3 red capsicums
2.1 kg (4 lb 3 oz) frozen turkey
  hindquarters (legs with
  thighs), chopped
plain flour, seasoned with salt
  and freshly ground pepper
¼ cup (60 ml/2 fl oz) olive oil
60 g (2 oz) butter
¾ cup (185 ml/6 fl oz) chicken
  stock
¼ teaspoon chilli flakes
4 fresh sage leaves, chopped, or
  ½ teaspoon dried sage
2 cloves garlic, crushed
1 teaspoon finely grated lemon
  rind
150 g (5 oz) sliced pancetta, or
  thinly sliced bacon
1 sprig of rosemary
2 tablespoons chopped flat-leaf
  parsley

1 Preheat the grill to high. Cut the capsicums in half, then remove the seeds and membranes. Place the capsicum halves skin-side-up under the grill and cook for 5–8 minutes, or until the skin blackens and blisters. Transfer to a plastic bag, seal and allow to cool, then peel away the blackened skin. Cut the flesh into thick slices.
2 Thaw the turkey pieces in a single layer in the refrigerator. When they have thawed, pat the turkey pieces well with paper towels to remove all the excess moisture, then coat them well in the seasoned flour, dusting off any excess.
3 Heat the oil and butter in a large pan. Brown the turkey pieces in batches over medium-high heat, then drain the pan of excess oil.
4 Pour the chicken stock into the pan and stir well, scraping the base and side of the pan to mix in all the pan juices. Add the chilli flakes, sage, garlic and lemon rind and cook, stirring, for 1 minute.
5 Return all the turkey pieces to the pan. Cover with the grilled capsicum slices, then layer the pancetta over

the top to completely cover. Add the rosemary sprig, cover the pan and cook over low heat for 1 hour, or until the turkey is succulent, yet not falling off the bone.
6 Discard the rosemary sprig and transfer the pancetta, capsicum slices and turkey pieces to a serving plate. Cover and keep warm. If the sauce is a little thin, place it over high heat and simmer for 3–4 minutes to thicken. Stir in the chopped parsley, adjust the seasoning if necessary, then spoon the sauce around the turkey to serve.

Place the grilled capsicum halves in a plastic bag, seal and allow to cool.

In batches, brown the turkey in the hot oil and butter over medium-high heat.

Cover the turkey with the capsicum slices, then cover with the pancetta.

NUTRITION PER SERVE (6)
Protein 65 g; Fat 55 g; Carbohydrate 5 g;
Dietary Fibre 2 g; Cholesterol 345 mg;
4265 kJ (1020 cal)

COOK'S FILE

Note: Ask your butcher or poulterer to saw the frozen turkey into 1½ –2 cm (¾ inch) pieces for you.
Pancetta is an Italian unsmoked bacon, rolled and cured with salt and spices, sold in many delicatessens. As an alternative, you could use prosciutto in this recipe.
Serving suggestion: This dish is delicious with a creamy mashed potato or polenta.

Coat the thawed turkey pieces lightly in the seasoned flour.

Pour the chicken stock into the pan and stir well to mix in all the pan juices.

Stir the chopped flat-leaf parsley into the simmering pan juices.

TURKEY POT ROAST

Preparation time: 20 minutes
Total cooking time: 1 hour 15 minutes
Serves 6

1 kg (2 lb) frozen turkey breast
   roll
2 tablespoons oil
20 g (¾ oz) butter
1 onion, cut into wedges
½ cup (125 ml/4 fl oz) chicken
   stock
½ cup (125 ml/4 fl oz) white wine
300 g (10 oz) orange sweet
   potato, cut into 3 cm (1¼
   inch) pieces
2 zucchini, cut into 2 cm (¾ inch)
   slices
½ cup (160 g/5½ oz) redcurrant
   jelly
1 tablespoon cornflour

1 Preheat the oven to moderate
180°C (350°F/Gas 4). Thaw the
turkey according to the instructions
on the label. Remove the elasticised
string from the turkey and tie up
securely with string, at regular
intervals, to retain its shape.

2 Heat the oil and butter in a frying
pan over high heat, and brown the
turkey all over. Transfer the turkey
to a 2 litre casserole dish. Place the
onion wedges around the turkey, and
pour over the stock and wine. Cover
and bake for 40 minutes. Add the
sweet potato and bake for 10
minutes. Add the zucchini and bake
for a further 20 minutes.

3 Transfer the turkey and
vegetables to a plate and keep warm.
Strain the liquid into a small
saucepan. Stir in the redcurrant jelly.
Combine the cornflour and 1
tablespoon water, and stir until
smooth. Add gradually to the pan,
stirring until the mixture boils and
thickens. Slice the turkey and serve
with the vegetables and sauce.

NUTRITION PER SERVE
Protein 46 g; Fat 12 g; Carbohydrate 21 g;
Dietary Fibre 1.5 g; Cholesterol 104 mg;
1630 kJ (390 cal)

*Tie up the turkey with string to help
retain its shape during cooking.*

*Pour the stock and wine over the turkey
and onion wedges.*

*Strain the cooking liquid into a small
saucepan, and stir in the redcurrant jelly.*

*Gradually add the cornflour mixture to the
sauce, and stir until it boils and thickens.*

GINGERED DUCK CURRY

Preparation time: 30 minutes +
  30 minutes refrigeration + soaking
Total cooking time: 1 hour 30 minutes
Serves 4

1.8 kg (3 lb 10 oz) duck
1 clove garlic, crushed
1 teaspoon grated fresh ginger
1 tablespoon dark soy sauce
½ teaspoon sesame oil
8 dried Chinese mushrooms
5 cm (2 inch) piece fresh ginger,
  peeled and thinly sliced
2 tablespoons yellow curry paste
2 tablespoons chopped lemon
  grass, white part only
400 ml (13 fl oz) can coconut
  milk

4 Kaffir lime leaves, shredded
100 g (3½ oz) Thai pea eggplants
2 teaspoons soft brown sugar
2 teaspoons fish sauce
1 tablespoon lime juice

1 Cut the duck in half by cutting down both sides of the backbone, through the breastbone. Discard the backbone. Cut each duck half into 4 portions, removing any fat. Rub the duck with the combined garlic, ginger, soy sauce and oil. Refrigerate for 30 minutes.

2 Soak the mushrooms in boiling water for 20 minutes. Drain, remove the stalks and cut in half.

3 Heat a lightly oiled pan. Brown the duck over medium heat. Leaving only 1 tablespoon of fat in the pan, stir-fry the ginger, curry paste and lemon grass for 3 minutes. Stir in the coconut milk, lime leaves and ½ cup (125 ml/4 fl oz) water. Add the duck; cover and simmer gently for 45 minutes. Skim well.

4 Remove the eggplant stems; add the eggplants to the pan with the sugar, fish sauce and mushrooms. Simmer, partly covered, for 30 minutes, or until tender. Stir in lime juice to taste.

NUTRITION PER SERVE (6)
Protein 50 g; Fat 40 g; Carbohydrate 6 g; Dietary Fibre 1 g; Cholesterol 300 mg; 2330 kJ (560 cal).

COOK'S FILE

NOTE: To reduce the fat in this dish, use light coconut milk and skin the duck.

Cut the duck down the middle. Cut the legs and breasts in half to give 8 portions.

Stir the coconut milk, water and lime leaves into the stir-fried spice mixture.

Remove the stems from the pea eggplants and add the eggplants to the pan.

RED WINE AND PORK STEW

Preparation time: 30 minutes +
  overnight marinating
Total cooking time: 1 hour 30 minutes
Serves 4–6

750 g (1½ lb) pork, cut into 3 cm
  (1¼ inch) cubes
¼ cup (60 ml/2 fl oz) oil
plain flour, seasoned with salt
  and freshly ground pepper
12 bulb spring onions, trimmed
3 rashers bacon, cut into strips
2 carrots, chopped
200 g (6½ oz) button mushrooms
2 sticks celery, sliced

1½ cups (375 ml/12 fl oz) chicken
  stock
1 teaspoon thyme leaves
1 tablespoon chopped parsley

Marinade
1 cup (250 ml/8 fl oz) red wine
1 tablespoon olive oil
4 cloves garlic, crushed
1 tablespoon thyme leaves
2 teaspoons rosemary leaves
2 tablespoons chopped parsley

1 Combine the marinade ingredients in a large bowl. Add the pork and mix well. Cover and refrigerate overnight.
2 Reserving the marinade, drain the pork. Heat 2 tablespoons of the oil in a large, deep saucepan. Coat the pork in the flour and brown in batches over high heat. Remove and set aside.
3 Heat the remaining oil. Cook the onions and bacon over medium-high heat for 5 minutes. Add the carrots, mushrooms and celery and cook for 5 minutes, stirring constantly.
4 Add pork, chicken stock and reserved marinade. Bring to the boil, then reduce heat and simmer for 1¼ to 1½ hours, or until pork is very tender, stirring often to prevent sticking. Season well with salt and pepper. Stir in the herbs and serve.

NUTRITION PER SERVE (6)
Protein 35 g; Fat 15 g; Carbohydrate 3.5 g; Dietary Fibre 3 g; Cholesterol 70 mg; 1340 kJ (320 cal)

Combine the marinade ingredients and the pork in a large bowl.

Lightly coat the drained pork in the seasoned flour.

Add the reserved marinade to the meat and vegetables.

PORK AND EGGPLANT POT

Preparation time: 20 minutes
Total cooking time: 1 hour 40 minutes
Serves 4

olive oil, for cooking
375 g (12 oz) slender eggplant,
    cut into 3 cm (1¼ inch) slices
8 bulb spring onions
400 g (13 oz) can chopped
    tomatoes
2 cloves garlic, crushed
2 teaspoons ground cumin
500 g (1 lb) pork fillet, sliced 3
    cm (1¼ inches) thick
plain flour, seasoned with salt
    and freshly ground pepper
⅔ cup (170 ml/5½ fl oz) cider

1 sprig of rosemary
2 tablespoons finely chopped
    toasted almonds

1 Heat 3 tablespoons of oil in a large, heavy-based pan. Brown the eggplant in batches over high heat, adding oil as needed. Remove and set aside.

2 Quarter the spring onions along their length. Add some oil to the pan and fry over medium heat for 5 minutes. Add the tomatoes, garlic and cumin; cook for 2 minutes. Remove and set aside.

3 Coat the pork in the flour, shaking off any excess. Brown in batches over medium-high heat until golden, adding oil as needed. Remove and set aside.

4 Add the cider to the pan and stir well, scraping down the side and base.

Allow to boil for 1–2 minutes, then add ½ cup (125 ml/4 fl oz) water. Reduce the heat and stir in the spring onions and tomatoes. Add the pork, season to taste and poke the rosemary sprig into the stew. Partially cover and simmer gently for 20 minutes.

5 Layer the eggplant on top, partially cover and cook for 25 minutes, or until the pork is tender. Just before serving, gently toss the almonds through.

NUTRITION PER SERVE
Protein 30 g; Fat 7 g; Carbohydrate 10 g; Dietary Fibre 5 g; Cholesterol 60 mg; 980 kJ (235 cal)

COOK'S FILE

Serving suggestion: This dish is lovely with a Cauliflower and fennel purée.

Fry the eggplant in batches over high heat until browned on both sides.

Add the cider to the frying pan, scraping the brown bits from the side and base.

Layer the eggplant over the top of the pork and tomato mixture.

HEARTY PORK AND RED LENTILS

Preparation time: 35 minutes
Total cooking time: 2 hours
Serves 4–6

1 kg (2 lb) lean pork neck, sliced
2 cm (¾ inch) thick
plain flour, seasoned with salt
and freshly ground pepper
50 g (1¾ oz) butter
1 tablespoon olive oil
1 large onion, finely chopped
3 cloves garlic, finely chopped
2 tablespoons chopped sage
1¼ cups (310 ml/10 fl oz)
vegetable stock
1¼ cups (310 ml/10 fl oz) red
wine
1 cup (250 g/8 oz) red lentils,
rinsed
2 carrots, chopped
2 potatoes, chopped
3 sticks celery, chopped
1 bay leaf, torn in three
2 teaspoons finely grated lemon
rind
2 tablespoons chopped parsley

1 Coat the pork in the flour, shaking off any excess. In a large, deep, heavy-based pan, heat the butter and oil over medium heat until foamy. Brown the pork well, in batches if necessary.
2 Return all the pork to the pan. Add the onion, garlic, sage, stock and wine; season well. Bring to the boil, turning the pork to coat in the liquid. Reduce the heat, cover and simmer for 1 hour, turning the pork during cooking. If the sauce becomes too thick, add about 1 cup (250 ml/8 fl oz) of water.

3 Add the lentils, carrots, potatoes, celery and bay leaf to the stew with 2 cups (500 ml/16 fl oz) of water, and plenty of salt and pepper. Bring to the boil, then reduce the heat to low. Simmer, covered, for 40 minutes.
4 Add the rind. Cook, uncovered, for 30 minutes, or until the sauce is thick and mash-like. If the pork is falling apart, remove and keep warm.

To serve, pile the sauce onto the plates, rest some pork on top and sprinkle with parsley. Serve with mashed potato and steamed green beans.

NUTRITION PER SERVE (6)
Protein 50 g; Fat 13 g; Carbohydrate 20 g; Dietary Fibre 8 g; Cholesterol 110 mg; 1884 kJ (450 cal)

Brown the pork well in the foamy butter and oil mixture.

When the wine mixture boils, turn the pork over to coat in the cooking liquid.

Add the lemon rind to the stew and cook, covered, for 30 minutes.

BRAISED PORK WITH PRUNES

Preparation time: 15 minutes
Total cooking time: 30 minutes
Serves 4

4 lean pork loin medallions,
    about 175 g (6 oz) each
2 cups (500 ml/16 fl oz) chicken
    stock
2 tablespoons oil
1 large onion, cut into wedges
2 cloves garlic, crushed
1 tablespoon fresh thyme leaves
1 large tomato, peeled, seeded
    and finely chopped
½ cup (125 ml/4 fl oz) cream
16 pitted prunes

1 Shape the meat into rounds by securing a length of string around the medallions. Tie with a bow for easy removal. Bring the stock to the boil in a medium saucepan. Reduce the heat to a simmer and cook for 5 minutes, or until reduced to ¾ cup (185 ml/6 fl oz).

2 Heat the oil over high heat in a heavy-based frying pan. Cook the meat for 2 minutes each side to seal, turning once. Drain on paper towels.

3 Add the onion and garlic to the saucepan, and stir for 2 minutes. Return the meat to the pan with the thyme, tomato and stock, then reduce the heat to low. Cover the pan and bring slowly to simmering point. Simmer for 10 minutes, or until the meat is tender, turning once. Add the cream and prunes, and simmer for a further 5 minutes.

NUTRITION PER SERVE
Protein 45 g; Fat 25 g; Carbohydrate 20 g; Dietary Fibre 4 g; Cholesterol 138 mg; 2015 kJ (480 cal)

Shape the pork medallions into rounds by securing a length of string around each one.

Cook the medallions in the oil for 2 minutes on each side, turning once.

Return the meat to the pan with the thyme, tomato and stock.

ITALIAN SAUSAGE AND CHICKPEA STEW

Preparation time: 15 minutes
Total cooking time: 45 minutes
Serves 4

2 large red capsicums
1 tablespoon olive oil
2 large red onions, cut into thick
  wedges
2 cloves garlic, finely chopped
600 g (1¼ lb) Italian-style thin
  pork sausages
300 g (10 oz) can chickpeas,
  drained
150 g (5 oz) flat mushrooms,
  thickly sliced
½ cup (125 ml/4 fl oz) dry white
  wine

2 bay leaves
2 teaspoons chopped fresh
  rosemary
400 g (13 oz) can diced tomatoes

1 Cut the capsicums into large pieces, removing the seeds and membrane. Place skin-side up, under a hot grill until the skin blackens and blisters. Allow to cool in a plastic bag. Peel away the skin, and slice diagonally into thick strips.
2 Meanwhile, heat the oil in a large non-stick frying pan. Add the onion and garlic, and stir over medium heat for 6 minutes, or until the onion is soft. Remove onion from pan and set aside. Add the sausages to the same pan. Cook over medium heat, turning occasionally, for 8 minutes, or until the sausages are browned. Remove

sausages from the pan and slice diagonally into 3 cm (1¼ inch) pieces.
3 Combine the capsicum slices, onion, sausage pieces, chickpeas and mushrooms in the pan, and cook over medium–high heat.
4 Add the wine, bay leaves and rosemary to the pan. Bring to the boil, then reduce the heat to low and simmer for 3 minutes. Stir in the tomato and simmer for 20 minutes, or until the sauce has thickened slightly. Remove bay leaves and season to taste with sugar, salt and pepper.

NUTRITION PER SERVE
Protein 20 g; Fat 25 g; Carbohydrate 25 g; Dietary Fibre 9.5 g; Cholesterol 50 mg; 1695 kJ (405 cal)

Grill the capsicums under a hot grill until the skin blackens and blisters.

Remove the skin from the cooked capsicums and slice them into thin strips.

Use a pair of tongs to hold the sausages as you cut them into short pieces.

HAM, LEEK AND POTATO RAGU

Preparation time: 25 minutes
Total cooking time: 45 minutes
Serves 4–6

50 g (1¾ oz) butter
2 tablespoons olive oil
250 g (8 oz) piece double-smoked
　ham, cut into cubes
3 cloves garlic, finely chopped
3 leeks, sliced
1.5 kg (3 lb) potatoes, peeled and
　cut into large chunks

2 cups (500 ml/16 fl oz) chicken
　stock
2 tablespoons brandy
½ cup (125 ml/4 fl oz) cream
1 tablespoon each of chopped
　fresh oregano and parsley

1 Heat the butter and oil in a large heavy-based saucepan. Cook the ham, garlic and leek over low heat for 10 minutes, stirring regularly.
2 Add the potato and cook for 10 minutes, stirring regularly.
3 Slowly stir in the combined stock and brandy. Cover and bring to a gentle simmer. Cook for another

15–20 minutes, or until the potato is very tender but still chunky, and the sauce has thickened. Add the cream and herbs, and season with salt and pepper. Simmer for another 5 minutes. Serve with toast.

NUTRITION PER SERVE (6)
Protein 15 g; Fat 25 g; Carbohydrate 40 g; Dietary Fibre 9 g; Cholesterol 70 mg; 1990 kJ (475 cal)

NOTE: You can use any type of ham for this recipe. A double-smoked ham will give a good flavour.

Heat the butter and oil in a pan, then cook the ham, garlic and leek.

Stir in the stock and brandy, then cover and leave to simmer.

Once the sauce has thickened, add the cream and chopped herbs.

PORK SAUSAGE AND WHITE BEAN STEW

Preparation time: 25 minutes +
 overnight soaking
Total cooking time: 1 hour 40 minutes
Serves 4

350 g (11 oz) dried white haricot
 beans
150 g (5 oz) tocino, speck or
 pancetta, unsliced
½ leek, thinly sliced
2 cloves garlic
1 bay leaf
1 small fresh red chilli, halved
 and seeded
1 small onion
2 cloves
1 sprig fresh rosemary
3 sprigs fresh thyme
1 sprig fresh parsley
¼ cup (60 ml/2 fl oz) olive oil
8 pork sausages
½ onion, finely chopped
1 green capsicum, finely chopped
½ teaspoon paprika
½ cup (125 ml/4 fl oz) tomato
 purée
1 teaspoon cider vinegar

1 Soak the beans overnight in cold water. Drain and rinse the beans under cold water. Put them in a large saucepan with the tocino, leek, garlic, bay leaf and chilli. Stud the onion with the cloves and add to the saucepan. Tie the rosemary, thyme and parsley together, and add to the saucepan. Pour in 3 cups (750 ml/24 fl oz) cold water and bring to the boil. Add 1 tablespoon of the oil, reduce the heat and simmer, covered, for about 1 hour, or until the beans are tender. When necessary, add a little more boiling water to keep the beans covered.

2 Prick each sausage 5 or 6 times and twist tightly in opposite directions in the middle to give 2 short fat sausages joined in the middle. Put in a single layer in a large frying pan and add enough cold water to reach halfway up their sides. Bring to the boil and simmer, turning two or three times, until all the water has evaporated and the sausages brown lightly in the little fat that is left in the pan. Remove from the pan and cut the short sausages apart. Add the remaining oil, the chopped onion and green capsicum to the pan, and fry over medium heat for 5–6 minutes. Stir in the paprika, cook for 30 seconds, then add the tomato purée. Season to taste. Cook, stirring, for 1 minute.

3 Remove the tocino, herb sprigs and any loose large pieces of onion from the bean mixture. Leave in any loose leaves from the herbs and any small pieces of onion. Add the sausages and sauce to the pan, and stir the vinegar through. Bring to the boil. Adjust the seasoning.

NUTRITION PER SERVE
Protein 39 g; Fat 51 g; Carbohydrate 43 g; Dietary Fibre 20 g; Cholesterol 99 mg; 3195 kJ (765 cal)

Twist each sausage in opposite directions so that it forms two short fat sausages.

Cook until all the water has evaporated and the sausages are lightly browned.

BOSTON BAKED BEANS

Preparation time: 25 minutes + 6–8
  hours soaking
Total cooking time: 1 hour 35 minutes
Serves 4–6

1¾ cups (350 g/11 oz) dried
  cannellini beans
1 whole ham hock
2 onions, chopped
2 tablespoons tomato paste
1 tablespoon Worcestershire
  sauce
1 tablespoon molasses
1 teaspoon French mustard
¼ cup (45 g/1½ oz) brown sugar
½ cup (125 ml/4 fl oz) tomato
  juice

1 Cover the beans with cold water
and soak for 6–8 hours, or overnight.
2 Drain the beans, rinse them well
and place in a large pan. Add the ham
hock and cover with cold water.
Bring to the boil, then reduce the
heat and simmer, covered, for 25
minutes, or until the beans are
tender. Preheat the oven to warm
160°C (315°F/Gas 2–3).
3 Remove the ham hock from the pan
and set aside to cool. Drain the beans,
reserving 1 cup (250 ml/8 fl oz) of the
cooking liquid. Trim the ham of all
skin, fat and sinew, then roughly chop
the meat and discard the bone.
4 Transfer the meat and beans to a 2
litre casserole dish. Add the reserved
liquid and all remaining ingredients.
Mix gently, then cover and bake for 1
hour. Serve with hot, buttered toast.

NUTRITION PER SERVE (6)
Protein 28 g; Fat 5 g; Carbohydrate 30 g;
Dietary Fibre 2 g; Cholesterol 60 mg;
1090 kJ (260 cal)

COOK'S FILE

Notes: Any type of dried bean can be
used in this recipe.
1 To quick-soak beans, place them in
a pan, add hot water to cover, bring
slowly to the boil, then remove from
the heat. Leave to soak for 1 hour
before draining and using.
• Cooked beans can be frozen in 1
cup quantities and thawed as
required.

*Place the drained beans in a large pan. Add
the ham hock and cover with cold water.*

*Trim the ham of all fat, skin and sinew,
then roughly chop the meat.*

*Add the reserved liquid and remaining
ingredients to the meat and beans.*

PORK AND MUSTARD STEW

Preparation time: 15 minutes
Total cooking time: 1 hour 10 minutes
Serves 4–6

2 tablespoons oil
1 kg (2 lb) pork neck, cut into 3 cm (1¼ inch cubes)
20 g (¾ oz) butter
1 large onion, sliced
1 clove garlic, crushed

250 g (8 oz) button mushrooms, halved
1 tablespoon plain flour
⅓ cup (80 ml/2¾ fl oz) lemon juice
1 cup (250 ml/8 fl oz) chicken stock
2 tablespoons wholegrain mustard
2 teaspoons honey
½ teaspoon ground cumin

1 Preheat the oven to warm 170°C (325°F/Gas 3). Heat the oil in a large, heavy-based pan and brown the pork in batches over high heat. Transfer to a large casserole dish.

2 Add the butter to the pan and cook the onion and garlic until soft but not brown. Add the mushrooms and cook for 1 minute. Stir in the flour, then the remaining ingredients. Stirring, bring to the boil. Season to taste and spoon the mixture over the pork. Cover and bake for 45 minutes, or until tender.

NUTRITION PER SERVE (6)
Protein 40 g; Fat 10 g; Carbohydrate 5 g; Dietary Fibre 2 g; Cholesterol 85 mg; 1195 kJ (285 cal)

Using a sharp knife, cut the pork neck into large cubes.

In the same pan, melt the butter, add the onion and garlic and cook until soft.

Stir the flour into the onion and garlic mixture. Add the remaining ingredients.

PORK WITH SOUR CHERRIES

Preparation time: 15 minutes
Total cooking time: 1 hour 35 minutes
Serves 4

1.5 kg (3 lb) pork neck (pork
    scotch fillet)
plain flour, seasoned with salt
    and freshly ground pepper
¼ cup (60 ml/2 fl oz) olive oil
30 g (1 oz) butter
2 onions, sliced
½ cup (125 ml/4 fl oz) chicken
    stock
½ cup (125 ml/4 fl oz) red wine
2 tablespoons chopped tarragon
    leaves
700 g (1 lb 7 oz) jar pitted
    cherries, syrup reserved

1 Preheat the oven to warm 160°C
(315°F/Gas 2–3). Cut pork into 4 cm
(1½ inch) cubes and toss lightly in the
seasoned flour, shaking off any excess.
Heat the oil in a large heavy-based
pan. In batches, quickly brown the
pork over medium heat and transfer to
a large, shallow casserole dish.
2 Melt the butter in the pan. Cook
the onion over low heat for 10
minutes, or until soft but not brown.
3 Add the stock, wine, tarragon and
1 cup (250 ml/8 fl oz) of the reserved
cherry syrup. Stirring, bring to the
boil and season to taste. Pour the
mixture over the pork, then cover and
bake for 1 hour. Drain the cherries,
stir them through the mixture and
bake for 15 minutes to heat through.

NUTRITION PER SERVE
Protein 90 g; Fat 25 g; Carbohydrate 30 g;
Dietary Fibre 4 g; Cholesterol 190 mg;
3050 kJ (730 cal)

*Add the pork to the hot oil and cook over
medium heat until well browned.*

*Add the onions to the melted butter and
cook until soft but not brown.*

*Add the stock, wine, tarragon and the
cherry syrup to the softened onions.*

PORK VINDALOO

Preparation time: 20 minutes
Total cooking time: 2 hours
Serves 4

¼ cup (60 ml/2 fl oz) oil
1 kg (2 lb) pork fillets, cut into
  bite-size pieces
2 onions, finely chopped
4 cloves garlic, finely chopped
1 tablespoon finely chopped fresh
  ginger
1 tablespoon garam masala
2 teaspoons brown mustard
  seeds
4 tablespoons vindaloo paste

1 Heat the oil in a saucepan, add the pork in small batches and cook over medium heat for 5–7 minutes, or until browned. Remove from the pan.
2 Add the onion, garlic, ginger, garam masala and mustard seeds to the pan, and cook, stirring, for 5 minutes, or until the onion is soft.
3 Return all the meat to the pan, add the vindaloo paste and cook, stirring, for 2 minutes. Add 2½ cups (625 ml/21 fl oz) water and bring to the boil. Reduce the heat and simmer, covered, for 1½ hours, or until the meat is tender. Serve with boiled rice and pappadums.

NUTRITION PER SERVE
Protein 58 g; Fat 20 g; Carbohydrate 4 g;
Dietary Fibre 2 g; Cholesterol 125 mg;
1806 kJ (430 cal)

Trim the pork of any excess fat or sinew and cut into cubes.

Cook the pork in small batches over medium heat until browned.

Add the vindaloo paste to the pan, and cook until the meat is tender.

VEAL, LEMON AND CAPER STEW

Preparation time: 30 minutes
Total cooking time: about 2 hours
Serves 4–6

1 tablespoon olive oil
50 g (1¾ oz) butter
1 kg (2 lb) stewing veal, cut into
    4 cm (1¼ inch) chunks
300 g (10 oz) French shallots
3 leeks, cut into large chunks
2 cloves garlic, crushed
1 tablespoon plain flour
2 cups (500 ml/16 fl oz) chicken
    stock
1 teaspoon grated lemon rind
⅓ cup (80 ml/2¾ fl oz) lemon
    juice
2 bay leaves
2 tablespoons capers, drained
    and well rinsed
chopped parsley, for serving
caper berries, to garnish

1 Preheat the oven to moderate
180°C (350°F/Gas 4). Heat the oil
and half the butter in a large, heavy-
based pan. Brown the veal in batches
over medium-high heat and transfer
to a large casserole dish.
2 Blanch the shallots in boiling water
for 30 seconds, then peel and add to
the pan with the leeks. Gently cook
for 5 minutes, or until soft and golden.
Add the garlic, cook for 1 minute,
then transfer to the casserole dish.
3 Melt the remaining butter in the
pan, add the flour and cook for 30
seconds. Remove from the heat, add
the stock and stir until well combined.
Return to the heat and cook, stirring,
until the sauce begins to bubble.
4 Pour the sauce into the casserole
dish and stir in the lemon rind,
lemon juice and bay leaves. Cover
and bake for 1–1½ hours, or until the
veal is tender. During the last 20
minutes of cooking, remove the lid to
allow the sauces to reduce a little.
5 To serve, stir in the capers and
season with salt and freshly cracked
black pepper. Sprinkle with parsley
and garnish with caper berries.

NUTRITION PER SERVE (6)
Protein 40 g; Fat 13 g; Carbohydrate 5 g;
Dietary Fibre 2 g; Cholesterol 160 mg;
1300 kJ (300 cal)

COOK'S FILE

Notes: Caper berries are sold in jars
of brine or vinegar in speciality
stores. l If possible, use tiny capers
in this dish as they have a superb
flavour. Regular capers can be used
instead.

*Add the leeks and peeled shallots to the
pan and gently fry until soft and golden.*

*Remove the pan from the heat and stir in
the stock, scraping up the brown bits.*

PAPRIKA VEAL WITH CARAWAY NOODLES

Preparation time: 10 minutes
Total cooking time: 1 hour 35 minutes
Serves 4

¼ cup (60 ml/2 fl oz) oil
1 kg (2 lb) veal shoulder, diced
1 large onion, thinly sliced
3 cloves garlic, finely chopped
¼ cup (60 g/2 oz) Hungarian paprika
½ teaspoon caraway seeds
2 x 400 g (13 oz) cans chopped tomatoes, one drained
350 g (11 oz) fresh fettuccine
40 g (1¼ oz) butter, softened

1 Heat half the oil in a large saucepan over medium–high heat, then brown the veal in batches for 3 minutes per batch. Remove the veal from the pan and set aside with any pan juices.
2 Add the remaining oil to the pan and sauté the onion and garlic over medium heat for 5 minutes, or until softened. Add the paprika and ¼ teaspoon of the caraway seeds, and stir for 30 seconds.
3 Add the chopped tomatoes and their liquid plus ½ cup (125 ml/4 fl oz) water. Return the veal to the pan with any juices, increase the heat to high and bring to the boil. Reduce the heat to low, then cover and simmer for 1¼ hours, or until the meat is tender and the sauce has thickened.

4 About 15 minutes before the veal is ready, cook the pasta in a large saucepan of rapidly boiling salted water according to the packet instructions until al dente. Drain, then return to the pan. Stir in the butter and the remaining caraway seeds. Serve immediately with the paprika veal.

NUTRITION PER SERVE
Protein 68 g; Fat 25 g; Carbohydrate 73 g; Dietary Fibre 10 g; Cholesterol 231 mg; 3340 kJ (800 cal)

Brown the veal in batches over medium–high heat for 3 minutes.

Cover and simmer until the meat is tender and the sauce has thickened.

VEAL WITH ALMONDS AND MUSHROOMS

Preparation time: 20 minutes
Total cooking time: 1 hour 50 minutes
Serves 4–6

75 g (2½ oz) blanched almonds
olive oil, for cooking
2 onions, chopped
1 kg (2 lb) diced veal
plain flour, seasoned with salt
    and freshly ground pepper
½ cup (125 ml/4 fl oz) red wine
500 g (1 lb) very ripe tomatoes,
    chopped
2 tablespoons chopped oregano
50 g (1¾ oz) butter
400 g (13 oz) mushrooms (such
    as tiny buttons, shiitake or
    porcini)

1 Preheat the oven to slow 150°C (300°F/Gas 2). Scatter the almonds on a baking tray and bake for 10 minutes, or until golden. Cool and roughly chop.
2 Heat 2 tablespoons of oil in a deep, heavy-based pan. Cook the onion over low heat for 15 minutes, stirring often. Remove and set aside, leaving as much oil as possible in the pan.
3 Toss the veal in the flour, shaking off any excess. Reheat the pan and brown the veal over medium heat in batches, adding more oil if necessary.
4 Return all the veal to the pan with any juices; add the onion and wine. Bring to the boil and stir well. Reduce the heat to very low, cover with foil and a tightly fitting lid, then simmer very gently for 1 hour.
5 Stir well, then mix in the tomatoes and oregano. Cover and simmer for another 20 minutes. Season to taste.

6 Melt the butter until foamy in a frying pan over medium heat. Cut any large mushrooms and cook until just wilted, tossing well.
7 To serve, dish the stew onto serving plates, top with the mushrooms, drizzle over any juices and sprinkle with the chopped toasted almonds.

NUTRITION PER SERVE (6)
Protein 45 g; Fat 17 g; Carbohydrate 6 g; Dietary Fibre 4 g; Cholesterol 160 mg; 1565 kJ (375 cal)

Gently cook the onion for 15 minutes, or until golden. Remove and set aside.

Return the browned veal to the pan with any juices. Add the onions and red wine.

When the butter is foaming, add all the mushrooms and cook until just wilted.

OSSO BUCO WITH GREMOLATA AND MILANESE RISOTTO

Preparation time: 40 minutes
Total cooking time: 2 hours 20 minutes
Serves 4

Gremolata
1 tablespoon finely shredded or zested lemon rind
1–2 cloves garlic, finely chopped
¼ cup (7 g/¼ oz) finely chopped parsley

Osso Buco
4 veal shank pieces, each 5 cm (2 inches) thick
plain flour, seasoned with salt and freshly ground pepper
2 tablespoons olive oil
2 large onions, sliced
6 egg tomatoes, finely chopped
2 tablespoons tomato paste
1½ cups (375 ml/12 fl oz) white wine
1 tablespoon cornflour
2–3 cloves garlic, crushed
1 cup (30 g/1 oz) finely chopped parsley

Milanese Risotto
1 litre chicken stock
50 g (1¾ oz) butter
2 tablespoons olive oil
1 onion, finely chopped
1–2 cloves garlic, crushed
¼ teaspoon saffron threads
1¼ cups (250 g/8 oz) arborio rice
½ cup (50 g/1⅔ oz) freshly grated Parmesan

1 To make the gremolata, combine the lemon rind, garlic and parsley and set aside.
2 Coat the veal with seasoned flour, shaking off any excess. Heat half the oil in a heavy-based pan large enough to fit the meat in a single layer. When the oil is hot, brown the veal well on all sides. Remove and set aside.
3 Heat the remaining oil in the pan and cook the onion for 2–3 minutes, or until soft but not brown. Add the meat in a single layer, sitting snugly in the pan. Season to taste.
4 Mix together the chopped tomatoes, tomato paste and wine and pour over the meat. Bring to the boil,

reduce the heat, cover and simmer for 1½ hours.
5 Remove 1 cup (250 ml/8 fl oz) of the cooking liquid and allow to cool a little. Place the cornflour in a small bowl and whisk in the liquid, then stir in the garlic and chopped parsley and add the mixture to the dish. Simmer, uncovered, for about 30 minutes, or until the meat is very tender and the sauce has thickened. Sprinkle with the gremolata just before serving.
6 While the sauce is simmering, make the risotto. Heat the stock in a pan and keep it at a simmer. In another heavy-based pan, heat the butter and oil. Add the onion, garlic

and saffron and cook, stirring, for 2–3 minutes without browning. Add the rice and stir for 1–2 minutes, or until well coated.
7 Add the stock, about ½ cup (125 ml/ 4 fl oz) at a time, stirring constantly over low heat until all the liquid is absorbed before adding more stock. Repeat until all the stock is absorbed and the rice is tender—this will take 25–30 minutes, and requires constant stirring. Stir in the Parmesan, season and serve at once.

NUTRITION PER SERVE
Protein 30 g; Fat 35 g; Carbohydrate 30 g; Dietary Fibre 5 g; Cholesterol 114 mg; 2580 kJ (615 cal)

To make the gremolata, combine the lemon rind, garlic and parsley.

When the oil is hot, brown the veal shanks well all over.

Pour the chopped tomatoes, tomato paste and wine over the meat and onions.

In a bowl, blend some of the cornflour with a cup of the cooled liquid.

Add the rice to the fried onion, garlic and saffron mixture; stir until coated.

Add the stock a little at a time, stirring until absorbed before adding more stock.

VEAL WITH SWEET VEGETABLES

Preparation time: 30 minutes
Total cooking time: 2 hours 30 minutes
Serves 4

olive oil, for cooking
8 veal shank pieces, each 2 cm
   (¾ inch) thick
2 cloves garlic, finely chopped
2 onions, chopped
2 carrots, chopped
1 stick celery, chopped
2 bay leaves, torn
750 ml (24 fl oz) beef stock
50 g (1¾ oz) butter
200 g (6½ oz) white sweet potato

200 g (6½ oz) parsnips
150 g (5 oz) baby turnips
150 g (5 oz) new potatoes
2 teaspoons soft brown sugar
2 tablespoons balsamic vinegar

1 Preheat the oven to warm 160°C (315°F/Gas 2–3). Heat 3 tablespoons of oil in a roasting pan over medium heat and brown the veal all over. Remove and set aside. Add the garlic, onion, carrot and celery and brown lightly for 10 minutes. Add the veal, bay leaves and stock and stir well. Bring to the boil, cover tightly with foil, then bake for 1½ hours.
2 Towards the end of baking, cut the sweet potato and parsnips into large chunks; trim the turnips and cut in

half. Heat the butter and a little oil in a deep frying pan until foamy. Toss all the root vegetables over medium heat for 5–6 minutes, or until the edges are golden. Sprinkle with sugar and vinegar and toss well. Cook gently for 10 minutes, or until the vegetables soften and the juices caramelise.
3 Turn the veal in the stock, add the vegetables and toss well. If the meat is drying out, stir in 1 cup (250 ml/8 fl oz) water. Season well, then cover and cook for 20 minutes. This dish is delicious served with steamed rice or creamy polenta.

NUTRITION PER SERVE
Protein 5 g; Fat 10 g; Carbohydrate 30 g; Dietary Fibre 6 g; Cholesterol 30 mg; 930 kJ (220 cal)

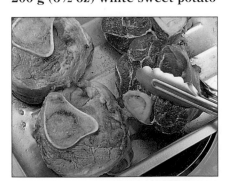

Heat the oil in a roasting pan, add the veal shanks and brown all over.

Add the root vegetables to the foaming butter. Cook until the edges are golden.

Add the caramelised vegetables to the veal mixture and toss well.

HUNGARIAN VEAL GOULASH

Preparation time: 20 minutes
Total cooking time: 2 hours
Serves 4

2 tablespoons olive oil
2 onions, chopped
500 g (1 lb) stewing veal, cubed
1 tablespoon Hungarian paprika
¼ teaspoon caraway seeds
425 g (14 oz) can tomatoes
2 cups (500 ml/16 fl oz) beef
    stock

1 large potato, diced
1 large carrot, thickly sliced
1 green capsicum, chopped
½ cup (125 g/4 oz) sour cream

1 Heat the oil in a large, heavy-based pan. Cook the onion for 10 minutes over medium heat, stirring from time to time, until soft and golden. Remove from the pan, increase the heat, then brown the veal in batches.
2 Return all the veal to the pan with the onion. Add the paprika, caraway seeds, chopped tomatoes and stock. Bring to the boil, reduce the heat, then cover and simmer for 1¼ hours.
3 Add the vegetables. Cook uncovered for 20 minutes, or until tender. Season to taste with salt and freshly cracked black pepper, and stir in the sour cream. Serve with rice or pasta.

NUTRITION PER SERVE
Protein 35 g; Fat 25 g; Carbohydrate 18 g; Dietary Fibre 5 g; Cholesterol 144 mg; 1805 kJ (430 cal)

COOK'S FILE

Note: Hungarian paprika is brighter and not as sweet as regular paprika.

Heat the oil and fry the onions over medium heat until soft and golden.

Add the paprika, caraway seeds, chopped tomatoes and stock to the fried onions.

Add the vegetables and cook, uncovered, for 20 minutes, or until tender.

In a bowl, combine the leeks, shallots, garlic, parsley, mint and zucchini.

Brush the veal with browned butter, then overlap a layer of veal over the vegetables.

Cut the bacon in half crossways and arrange over the top layer of vegetables.

Evenly pour the cream in around the edge of the dish.

SPRING VEAL WITH BACON AND ZUCCHINI

Preparation time: 20 minutes
Total cooking time: 1 hour 50 minutes
Serves 4–6

3 medium leeks, thinly sliced
6 French shallots, chopped
2 cloves garlic, crushed
2 tablespoons chopped parsley
2 tablespoons chopped mint
200 g (6½ oz) small young
    zucchini, thickly sliced
85 g (3 oz) butter
1 kg (2 lb) thin leg veal slices
4 rashers lean bacon
⅓ cup (80 ml/2½ fl oz) cream
4 baby zucchini, with flowers

1 Combine the leeks, shallots, garlic, parsley, mint and sliced zucchini. Spread a thin layer in a deep, oiled ovenproof dish; season well. Preheat the oven to warm 170°C (325°F/Gas 3).

2 Gently melt the butter in a pan until golden brown with a nutty aroma. Remove from the heat.
3 Cut the veal into 9 cm (3½ inch) pieces, brush with the browned butter and season well. Overlap a veal layer over the vegetables. Repeat the layers, finishing with a layer of vegetables.
4 Remove the rind from the bacon. Cut bacon in half crossways and arrange over vegetables. Cover and bake for 40 minutes. Pour cream in around the edge, then bake, partially covered, for 40 minutes more.
5 Arrange the baby zucchini over the bacon rashers. Cover and bake for 15–20 minutes: the vegetables and veal will shrink in from the sides of the dish to form a mould. If the sauce is thin, simmer in a pan until thick. Cut the mould into portions and drizzle with the sauce to serve.

NUTRITION PER SERVE (6)
Protein 50 g; Fat 20 g; Carbohydrate 3 g; Dietary Fibre 3 g; Cholesterol 200 mg; 1640 kJ (390 cal)

VEAL AND FENNEL CASSEROLE

Preparation time: 20 minutes
Total cooking time: 2 hours 15 minutes
Serves 4–6

1 tablespoon oil
30 g (1 oz) butter
4 veal shanks, cut into 4 cm (1½ inch) pieces
1 large onion, sliced
1 clove garlic, crushed
2 sticks celery, thickly sliced
3 carrots, thickly sliced
2 small fennel bulbs, quartered
⅓ cup (80 ml/2¾ fl oz) white wine
¼ cup (30 g/1 oz) plain flour
425 g (14 oz) can crushed tomatoes
1 cup (250 ml/8 fl oz) chicken stock
1 tablespoon chopped thyme
12 black olives

1 Preheat the oven to moderate 180°C (350°F/Gas 4). Heat the oil and butter in a large heavy-based pan and brown the meat quickly in batches on both sides over high heat. Transfer to a large, shallow casserole dish.
2 Add the onion and garlic to the pan and cook over medium heat until soft. Add the celery, carrot and fennel and cook for 2 minutes. Add the flour, stir until golden, then add the tomatoes, wine, stock and thyme. Bring to the boil, reduce the heat and simmer for 5 minutes, or until thickened. Season with salt and freshly ground pepper.
3 Add the sauce to the veal; cover and bake for 1½–2 hours, or until tender. Scatter with olives to serve.

NUTRITION PER SERVE (6)
Protein 20 g; Fat 8 g; Carbohydrate 10 g; Dietary Fibre 3 g; Cholesterol 80 mg; 840 kJ (200 cal)

COOK'S FILE

Note: Many butchers sell veal shanks already cut into pieces. You will need 12 medium pieces for this recipe.

Trim the leaves and base from the celery stalks and thickly cut the stalks.

Heat the oil and butter, then brown the meat in batches over high heat.

Add the celery, carrots and fennel to the onion and garlic and cook for 2 minutes.

Using sharp scissors, cut the forelegs off the rabbit through the connective tissue.

Cutting where the hind legs join the body, remove the legs and cut in half to separate.

Cut the ribcage and body of the rabbit into 4 even pieces.

Add the peeled and chopped tomatoes to the pan and simmer for 45 minutes.

COUNTRY RABBIT IN RED WINE

Preparation time: 15 minutes
Total cooking time: 1 hour 30 minutes
Serves 4

1.25 kg (2 lb 8 oz) rabbit
½ cup (125 ml/4 fl oz) olive oil
2 cloves garlic, crushed
1 sprig of rosemary, finely chopped
1 cup (250 ml/8 fl oz) red wine
½ cup (125 ml/4 fl oz) chicken stock
4 tomatoes, peeled and chopped

1 Cut the forelegs from the rabbit by cutting through the connective tissue joining the body. Cut across the back of the rabbit just above the legs, then cut the legs in half. Cut the body (saddle) of the rabbit into 2 pieces, then cut the ribcage and backbone into 4 pieces, to form 8 portions.

2 Heat the oil in a heavy-based pan. Add the rabbit, garlic and rosemary and brown the rabbit over medium heat on all sides.

3 Add the wine and stock; season with salt and freshly ground black pepper. Cover and simmer gently for 30 minutes. Add the tomatoes and cook, covered, for another 45 minutes over low heat, or until the rabbit is tender. Serve with crusty Italian bread to mop up the juices.

NUTRITION PER SERVE
Protein 75 g; Fat 40 g; Carbohydrate 4 g; Dietary Fibre 2 g; Cholesterol 190 mg; 3020 kJ (720 cal)

COOK'S FILE

Note: To save time, ask your butcher or poulterer to cut the rabbit for you.

RABBIT, CHORIZO AND OLIVE CASSEROLE

Preparation time: 35 minutes
Total cooking time: 2 hours 30 minutes
Serves 4–6

150 g (5 oz) French shallots
2 tablespoons olive oil
2 kg (4 lb) rabbit pieces
2 chorizo sausages, sliced
12 pickling onions
2 cloves garlic, crushed
1 teaspoon dried thyme
1 teaspoon paprika
1 tablespoon plain flour
½ cup (125 ml/4 fl oz) white wine
1½ cups (375 ml/12 fl oz) chicken stock
1 tablespoon tomato paste
½ teaspoon grated orange rind
⅓ cup (80 ml/2¾ fl oz) orange juice
12 Kalamata olives
2 tablespoons chopped parsley
2 tablespoons chopped chives

1 Soak the shallots in boiling water for 30 seconds; drain and peel. Preheat the oven to moderate 180°C (350°F/Gas 4).
2 In a large, heavy-based pan, heat half the oil and brown the rabbit in batches over high heat, then transfer to a large casserole dish. Heat the remaining oil; fry the chorizo, shallots and onions over medium heat until soft and golden.
3 Add the garlic, thyme and paprika and cook for 1 minute. Add the flour and cook for 30 seconds.

4 Remove from the heat, pour in the wine and stir well, scraping up any bits in the pan. Return to the heat, add the stock and stir until bubbling. Add the tomato paste, rind and orange juice, then add to the rabbit and mix well. Cover and cook for 2–2¼ hours, or until the rabbit is tender. Season to taste, stir in the olives and parsley and scatter with chives to serve.

NUTRITION PER SERVE (6)
Protein 95 g; Fat 28 g; Carbohydrate 12 g; Dietary Fibre 1.5 g; Cholesterol 264 mg; 3052 kJ (730 cal)

COOK'S FILE

NOTE: Chorizo is a spicy Spanish pork sausage flavoured with cayenne.

Place the shallots in a bowl and cover with boiling water, then drain and peel.

Heat the remaining oil in the pan and add the chorizo, shallots and onions.

Heat half the oil in a large pan. Brown the rabbit in batches over high heat.

SPICY VENISON AND VEGETABLE HOTPOT

Preparation time: 45 minutes
Total cooking time: 2 hours
Serves 6

1 tablespoon olive oil
25 g (¾ oz) butter
100 g (3½ oz) pancetta, chopped
1 kg (2 lb) trimmed shoulder of venison, cut into 4 cm (1½ inch) cubes
2 onions, each cut into 8 wedges
2 cloves garlic, crushed
1 tablespoon chopped fresh ginger
1 teaspoon ground cinnamon

½ teaspoon allspice
1 teaspoon dried thyme
1 bay leaf
500 g (1 lb) tomatoes, peeled, seeded and diced
1 cup (250 ml/8 fl oz) beef stock
⅓ cup (80 ml/2¾ fl oz) orange juice
⅓ cup (80 ml/2¾ fl oz) port
200 g (6½ oz) turnip
200 g (6½ oz) parsnip
200 g (6½ oz) carrot
chopped chives, to garnish

1 Heat the oil and butter in a large, heavy-based pan. Cook the pancetta over medium heat until lightly golden. Remove and set aside.
2 Brown the venison in batches and set aside. Cook the onion until golden; add the garlic and ginger and cook for 1 minute. Add the pancetta and venison and all ingredients except the root vegetables. Bring to the boil, then reduce the heat, cover tightly and very gently simmer for 1 hour.
3 Peel the turnip, parsnip and carrot, cut into even-sized wedges and add to the pan. Cover and cook for 40 minutes, or until tender, then uncover to reduce the sauce. Season to taste, scatter with the chives and serve.

NUTRITION PER SERVE
Protein 40 g; Fat 25 g; Carbohydrate 14 g; Dietary Fibre 5 g; Cholesterol 90 mg; 1895 kJ (460 cal)

Brown the venison in batches in the hot oil and butter.

Add the pancetta and venison with all the ingredients except the root vegetables.

Peel and cut the turnip, parsnip and carrot into wedges about the same size.

MOROCCAN SEAFOOD WITH CORIANDER

Preparation time: 50 minutes
Total cooking time: 50 minutes
Serves 6

2 tablespoons olive oil
2 red onions, roughly chopped
1 red capsicum, chopped
4 cloves garlic, crushed
2 teaspoons ground cumin
1 teaspoon ground coriander
2 teaspoons sweet paprika
½ teaspoon dried chilli flakes
1 cup (250 ml/8 fl oz) chicken or
  fish stock
425 g (14 oz) can chopped
  tomatoes
⅓ cup (80 ml/2¾ fl oz) orange
  juice
1 tablespoon sugar
¼ cup (40 g/1¼ oz) seedless
  raisins
375 g (12 oz) baby new potatoes
500 g (1 lb) baby octopus, cleaned
12 raw king prawns, peeled and
  deveined, tails intact
1 kg (2 lb) thick white fish fillets,
  cut into chunks

CORIANDER PUREE
1 cup (30 g/1 oz) fresh coriander
  leaves
2 tablespoons ground almonds
⅓ cup (80 ml/2¾ fl oz) extra
  virgin olive oil
½ teaspoon ground cumin
1 teaspoon honey

1 Heat the olive oil in a large saucepan and cook the onion over medium heat for about 5 minutes, or until soft. Add the capsicum and garlic, and cook for another minute. Add the cumin, coriander, paprika and chilli flakes, and cook until fragrant.
2 Pour in the stock, tomato, orange juice, sugar and raisins, and bring to the boil. Add the potatoes, reduce the heat to low and gently simmer for 20–30 minutes, or until the potatoes are just tender. Season to taste.
3 Use a small sharp knife to remove the octopus heads; slit the heads open and remove the gut. Grasp the body firmly and push the beak out with your index finger; remove and discard. Add the octopus, prawns and

fish to the pan and cook, covered, for 10 minutes, or until the fish flakes when tested with a fork.
4 To make the coriander purée, place the coriander leaves and ground almonds in a food processor. With the motor running, drizzle in the oil and process until smooth, then add the cumin, honey and salt to taste. Process until well combined.

5 To serve, dish the stew onto serving plates and drizzle a spoonful of purée on top. Serve with couscous and a green leaf salad.

NUTRITION PER SERVE
Protein 60 g; Fat 30 g; Carbohydrate 25 g; Dietary Fibre 4 g; Cholesterol 175 mg; 2415 kJ (580 cal)

Peel and devein the prawns, and cut the cleaned octopus into bite-sized pieces.

Process the coriander leaves and ground almonds, gradually drizzling in the oil.

SEAFOOD STEW WITH FETA AND OLIVES

Preparation time: 20 minutes
Total cooking time: 35 minutes
Serves 4

500 g (1 lb) fresh mussels
12 raw king prawns
750 g (1½ lb) firm white fish fillets
2 tablespoons olive oil
1 large onion, sliced
2 x 400 g (13 oz) cans tomatoes, chopped
2 strips lemon rind
1 tablespoon chopped lemon thyme
⅓ cup (80 ml/2¾ fl oz) dry vermouth or white wine
1 teaspoon sugar
12 black olives
125 g (4 oz) feta cheese, cubed

1 Discard any open mussels; scrub the rest and remove the beards. Place the mussels in a pan of simmering water: as soon as the shells open, place the mussels in a bowl of cold water, discarding any unopened ones. Open them up and leave on their half shells, discarding the other half.

2 Peel and devein the prawns, leaving the tails intact. Cut the fish into bite-sized pieces, removing any bones. Cover and refrigerate. Preheat the oven to moderate 180°C (350°F/Gas 4).

3 Heat the oil in a large, heavy-based pan and cook the onion over low heat for 5 minutes, or until soft but not brown. Add the tomatoes, lemon rind, lemon thyme, vermouth and sugar. Bring to the boil and season to taste. Reduce the heat, cover and simmer for 10 minutes.

4 Place the seafood in a shallow, ovenproof dish and cover with the hot sauce. Bake, covered, for 10 minutes. Add the remaining ingredients, covering the seafood with the sauce. Bake for 10 minutes, or until heated through. Serve immediately.

NUTRITION PER SERVE
Protein 70 g; Fat 25 g; Carbohydrate 10 g; Dietary Fibre 4 g; Cholesterol 313 mg; 2430 kJ (580 cal)

Scrub the mussels, remove the beards, then place in a pan of simmering water.

Peel and devein the prawns and cut the fish into bite-sized pieces.

Add the tomatoes, lemon rind, thyme, vermouth and sugar to the softened onion.

SEAFOOD MORNAY CASSEROLE

Preparation time: 25 minutes
Total cooking time: 40 minutes
Serves 4–6

400 g (13 oz) mussels
3 medium white fish fillets, cut
  into 3 cm (1¼ inch) cubes
250 g (8 oz) raw medium prawns,
  peeled and deveined
200 g (6½ oz) scallops, trimmed
1 small onion, halved
2 bay leaves
½ lemon, sliced
½ cup (125 ml/4 fl oz) white wine

SAUCE
45 g (1½ oz) butter
1 celery stick, chopped
1 large carrot, finely chopped
1½ tablespoons plain flour
1½ cups (375 ml/12 fl oz) milk
125 g (4 oz) Gruyère cheese,
  grated
1 cup (130 g/4½ oz) frozen peas

TOPPING
1 cup (80 g/2¾ oz) fresh
  breadcrumbs
½ cup (45 g/1½ oz) flaked
  almonds
2 teaspoons finely grated lemon
  rind
½ teaspoon freshly ground black
  pepper
60 g (2 oz) butter, chopped

1 Preheat the oven to moderate 180°C (350°F/Gas 4). Discard any open mussels, then remove the beards from the rest of the mussels and wash away any grit. Prise open the shells and remove the mussels.

Place the fish, prawns, scallops and mussels in a saucepan. Cover with cold water and add the onion, bay leaves, lemon and wine. Bring slowly to the boil. Cover, then reduce the heat to low and simmer for 3–4 minutes. Remove the seafood from the cooking liquid and place it in a lightly greased casserole dish.

2 To make the sauce, heat the butter in a saucepan. Cook the celery and carrot for 1 minute, then add the flour. Stir over low heat for 2 minutes, or until the mixture is lightly golden. Add the milk gradually, stirring until smooth. Stir constantly over medium heat for 3 minutes, or until the mixture boils and thickens. Boil for 1 minute, then remove from the heat and cool the sauce to room temperature.

3 Stir the cheese and peas into the sauce, then pour it over the seafood. Mix gently to combine.

4 To make the topping, combine the breadcrumbs, almonds, rind and pepper in a bowl. Spread evenly over the top of the seafood mixture. Dot with the butter. Bake for 20 minutes, or until the seafood is heated through and the top is golden brown.

NUTRITION PER SERVE (6)
Protein 42 g; Fat 31 g; Carbohydrate 18 g; Dietary Fibre 3 g; Cholesterol 177 mg; 2165 kJ (515 cal)

NOTE: Any combination of cooked seafood can be used in this recipe. The cooking liquid can replace half the milk, if desired.

Once the shells have been cleaned, prise them open and remove the mussels.

Heat the butter in a medium saucepan and cook the celery and carrot for 1 minute.

Pour the sauce over the seafood in the casserole dish, and mix gently to combine.

CATALAN FISH STEW

Preparation time: 30 minutes
Total cooking time: 40 minutes
Serves 6–8

300 g (10 oz) red mullet fillets
400 g (13 oz) firm white fish
    fillets
300 g (10 oz) cleaned calamari
1.5 litres fish stock
⅓ cup (80 ml/2¾ fl oz) olive oil
1 onion, chopped
6 cloves garlic, chopped
1 small fresh red chilli, chopped
1 teaspoon paprika
pinch saffron threads
150 ml (5 fl oz) white wine
425 g (14 oz) can crushed
    tomatoes
16 raw medium prawns, peeled
    and deveined, tails intact
2 tablespoons brandy
24 black mussels, cleaned
1 tablespoon chopped fresh
    parsley

PICADA
2 tablespoons olive oil
2 slices day-old bread, cubed
2 cloves garlic
5 blanched almonds, toasted
2 tablespoons fresh flat-leaf
    parsley

1 Cut the fish and calamari into 4 cm (1½ inch) pieces. Place the stock in a large saucepan, bring to the boil and boil for 15 minutes, or until reduced by half.
2 To make the picada, heat the oil in a frying pan, add the bread and cook, stirring, for 2–3 minutes, or until golden, adding the garlic for the last minute. Place the almonds, bread, garlic and parsley in a food processor and process, adding enough of the stock to make a smooth paste.
3 Heat 2 tablespoons of the oil in a large saucepan, add the onion, garlic, chilli and paprika, and cook, stirring, for 1 minute. Add the saffron, wine, tomato and stock. Bring to the boil, then reduce the heat and simmer.
4 Heat the remaining oil in a frying pan and quickly fry the fish and calamari for 3–5 minutes. Remove from the pan. Add the prawns, cook for 1 minute and then pour in the brandy. Carefully ignite the brandy with a match and let the flames burn down. Remove from the pan.
5 Add the mussels to the stock and simmer, covered, for 2–3 minutes, or until opened. Discard any that do not open. Add all the seafood and the picada to the pan, stirring until the sauce has thickened and the seafood has cooked through. Season to taste, sprinkle with the parsley, and serve.

NUTRITION PER SERVE (8)
Protein 26 g; Fat 18 g; Carbohydrate 5 g; Dietary Fibre 1.5 g; Cholesterol 136 mg; 1275 kJ (305 cal)

Process the almonds, bread, garlic, parsley and some of the stock to a smooth paste.

Quickly cook the fish and calamari in the oil in a frying pan.

Add the mussels to the stock and simmer until they open.

CIOPPINO

Preparation time: 30 minutes +
  30 minutes soaking
Total cooking time: 1 hour
Serves 4

2 dried mushrooms
1 kg (2 lb) firm white fish fillets
375 g (12 oz) raw king prawns
1 raw lobster tail
12 mussels
¼ cup (60 ml/2 fl oz) olive oil
1 large onion, finely chopped
1 green capsicum, finely chopped
2–3 cloves garlic, crushed
425 g (14 oz) can crushed
  tomatoes
1 cup (250 ml/8 fl oz) white wine
1 cup (250 ml/8 fl oz) tomato
  juice
1 cup (250 ml/8 fl oz) fish stock
bay leaf
2 sprigs of parsley
6 basil leaves, chopped
1 tablespoon chopped parsley

1 Soak the mushrooms for 20
minutes. Cut the fish into bite-size
pieces, removing any bones. Peel
and devein the prawns, leaving the
tails intact. Remove the meat from
the lobster shell and cut into small
pieces. Discard any open mussels;
scrub the rest, remove the beards,
then soak in cold water for 10
minutes. Drain the mushrooms,
squeeze dry and chop finely.
2 Heat the oil in a heavy-based pan.
Stirring, cook the onion, capsicum
and garlic over medium heat for about
5 minutes, or until the onion is soft.
Add the mushrooms, tomatoes, wine,
tomato juice, stock, bay leaf, parsley
sprigs and chopped basil. Bring to the

boil, reduce the heat, then cover and
simmer for 30 minutes.
3 Layer the fish and prawns in a
large pan. Add the sauce mixture,
then cover and leave on low heat for
10 minutes, or until the prawns are
pink and the fish is cooked. Add the
lobster and mussels and simmer for
2–3 minutes. Season to taste.
Discard any unopened mussels,
sprinkle with parsley, and serve with
crusty bread.

NUTRITION PER SERVE
Protein 100 g; Fat 25 g; Carbohydrate 8 g;
Dietary Fibre 3 g; Cholesterol 460 mg;
2905 kJ (695 cal)

COOK'S FILE

Note: You can make your own fish
stock for this recipe by simmering
the trimmings from the fish, lobster
and prawns in 1¼ cups (310 ml/10 fl
oz) of water for about 20 minutes,
then straining the liquid.

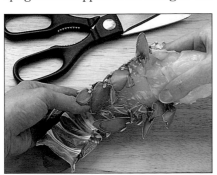

*Remove the lobster meat from the shell and
cut into small pieces.*

*When the onion is soft, add the chopped
mushroom, tomatoes, liquids and herbs.*

*Add the lobster and mussels when the
prawns are pink and the fish is cooked.*

Trim the ends from the fennel and slice the bulb thinly.

Add the Pernod and wine to the softened fennel, leek and garlic mixture.

SEAFOOD, FENNEL AND POTATO STEW

Preparation time: 10 minutes
Total cooking time: 30 minutes
Serves 6

1 large fennel bulb
2 tablespoons olive oil
2 leeks, thinly sliced
2 cloves garlic, crushed
½ teaspoon paprika
2 tablespoons Pernod or Ricard
200 ml (6½ fl oz) dry white wine
18 mussels, scrubbed and beards
    removed
¼ teaspoon saffron threads
¼ teaspoon thyme leaves
6 baby octopus
16 raw prawns, peeled and
    deveined
500 g (1 lb) swordfish steaks, cut
    into large chunks
400 g (13 oz) baby new potatoes
fennel greens, to garnish

1 Trim and thinly slice the fennel. Heat the oil in a large pan over medium heat. Add the fennel, leek and garlic. Stir in the paprika, season

lightly and cook for 8 minutes, or until softened. Add the Pernod and wine and stir for 1 minute, or until reduced by a third.
2 Add the mussels, discarding any open ones. Cover and cook for 1 minute or until opened, discarding any which do not. Remove from the pan to cool; remove from the shells and set aside.
3 Add the saffron and thyme to the pan and cook for 1–2 minutes, stirring. Adjust the seasoning and transfer to a large, flameproof casserole dish.
4 Use a small sharp knife to remove the octopus heads. Grasp the bodies and push the beaks out with your index finger; remove and discard. Slit the heads and remove the gut. Mix the octopus, prawns, fish and potatoes into the stew. Cover and cook gently for 10 minutes, or until tender. Add the mussels, cover and heat through. Garnish with fennel greens and serve.

NUTRITION PER SERVE
Protein 65 g; Fat 10 g; Carbohydrate 15 g; Dietary Fibre 5 g; Cholesterol 390 mg; 1840 kJ (440 cal)

When the mussels are cool, remove them from their shells.

Cut off the octopus heads. Grasp the body firmly and push out the beak.

TUNA AND WHITE BEAN CASSEROLE

Preparation time: 40 minutes +
  overnight soaking
Total cooking time: 3 hours
Serves 6

2 cups (400 g/13 oz) dried
  cannellini beans
¼ cup (60 ml/2 fl oz) olive oil
2 red onions, chopped
2 cloves garlic, crushed
1 teaspoon ground coriander
1 teaspoon finely grated lemon
  rind
2 teaspoons chopped fresh thyme
2 cups (500 ml/16 fl oz) white wine
2 cups (500 ml/16 fl oz) fish stock
475 g (15 oz) can tuna in brine,
  drained
1 bunch fresh basil, leaves only
4 large ripe tomatoes, cut into
  1 cm (½ inch) slices

TOPPING
½ cup (40 g/1¼ oz) fresh
  breadcrumbs
1 clove garlic, crushed
½ cup (30 g/1 oz) finely chopped
  fresh parsley
30 g (1 oz) butter, melted

1 Soak the beans in water overnight, then drain.
2 Heat the oil in a large, heavy-based saucepan. Add the onion, garlic, coriander, rind and thyme. Cook over medium heat for 10–15 minutes, or until the onion is softened. Add the beans and cook for 10 minutes.
3 Add the wine and stock. Cover and cook over low heat for 2 hours, until the beans are tender but not mashed.
4 Preheat the oven to hot 210°C (415°F/Gas 6–7). Transfer the bean mixture to a large casserole dish. Top with the tuna and basil leaves. Arrange tomato slices over the basil.
5 To make the topping, combine the breadcrumbs, garlic and parsley. Sprinkle over the tomato. Drizzle with the butter. Bake for 30 minutes, or until golden. Serve with crusty bread.

NUTRITION PER SERVE
Protein 32 g; Fat 16 g; Carbohydrate 36 g; Dietary Fibre 16 g; Cholesterol 41 mg; 1920 kJ (459 cal)

Add the drained cannellini beans to the onion mixture in the pan.

Add the wine and stock to the bean mixture, and cook for 2 hours.

Arrange the tuna pieces over the bean mixture in the casserole dish.

Lay the tomato slices over the basil leaves, then sprinkle with the topping.

ZARZUELA

Preparation time: 40 minutes
Total cooking time: 1 hour 10 minutes
Serves 4

Sofrito Sauce
1 tablespoon olive oil
2 onions, finely chopped
2 large tomatoes, peeled, seeded
   and chopped
1 tablespoon tomato paste

Picada Sauce
3 slices white bread, crusts
   removed
10 blanched almonds, toasted
3 cloves garlic
1 tablespoon olive oil

1 raw lobster tail
750 g (1½ lb) white boneless fish,
   cut into bite-size pieces
plain flour, seasoned with salt
   and freshly ground pepper
1 tablespoon olive oil
125 g (4 oz) calamari rings
12 raw king prawns
½ cup (125 ml/4 fl oz) white wine
12 mussels, scrubbed and beards
   removed

½ cup (125 ml/4 fl oz) brandy
¼ cup (15 g/½ oz) chopped
   parsley

1 To make the sofrito sauce, heat the oil in a pan over medium heat. Add the onion and cook, stirring, for 5 minutes without browning. Add the tomato, tomato paste and ½ cup (125 ml/4 fl oz) water and cook, stirring, over medium heat for a further 10 minutes. Stir in another ½ cup (125 ml/4 fl oz) water, season with salt and freshly ground pepper and set aside.

2 To make the picada sauce, finely chop the bread, almonds and garlic in a food processor. With the motor running, gradually add the oil to form a paste, adding another ½ tablespoon of oil if necessary.

3 Preheat the oven to moderate 180°C (350°F/Gas 4). Cut the lobster tail into rounds through the membrane that separates the shell segments. Set the rounds aside.

4 Lightly coat the fish in the flour. Heat the oil in a large pan and fry the fish over medium heat for 2–3 minutes, or until cooked and golden all over. Transfer to a large casserole dish.

5 Add the calamari to the pan and cook, stirring, for 1–2 minutes, then remove and add to the fish. Cook the lobster rounds and unshelled prawns for 2–3 minutes, or until just pink, then add to the casserole.

6 Add the wine to the pan and, when hot, add the mussels, discarding any which are already open. Cover and steam the mussels for 2–3 minutes. Discard any that do not open and add the rest to the casserole.

7 Ensuring nothing flammable is nearby, pour the brandy into one side of the pan and, when it has warmed, carefully ignite the brandy. Gently shake the pan until the flames have died down. Pour this mixture over the seafood in the casserole.

8 Pour over the sofrito sauce. Cover the casserole and bake for 20 minutes. Stir in the picada sauce and cook for a further 10 minutes, or until warmed through—do not overcook, or the seafood will toughen. Sprinkle with parsley to serve.

NUTRITION PER SERVE
Protein 90 g; Fat 30 g; Carbohydrate 15 g;
Dietary Fibre 4 g; Cholesterol 410 mg;
3095 kJ (790 cal)

Transfer the lightly fried seafood to the casserole dish.

Add the mussels to the hot wine. Cover and steam for 2–3 minutes.

Remove the mussels and carefully pour the brandy into one side of the pan.

Add the tomatoes, tomato paste and water to the softened onions.

Finely chop the bread, almonds and garlic in a food processor. Gradually add the oil.

Cut the lobster tail into rounds through the membrane, separating the shell segments.

BOUILLABAISSE

Preparation time: 30 minutes +
  5 minutes soaking
Total cooking time: 1 hour 15 minutes
Serves 6

¼ cup (60 ml/2 fl oz) olive oil
1 large onion, chopped
2 leeks, sliced
4 cloves garlic, crushed
500 g (1 lb) ripe tomatoes, peeled
  and roughly chopped
1–2 tablespoons tomato paste
6 sprigs fresh flat-leaf parsley
2 bay leaves
2 sprigs fresh thyme
1 sprig fresh fennel
¼ teaspoon saffron threads
2 kg (4 lb) seafood trimmings (fish
  heads, bones, shellfish remains)
1 tablespoon Pernod or Ricard
4 potatoes, cut into 1.5 cm (⅝
  inch) slices
1.5 kg (3 lb) fish fillets and
  steaks, such as blue-eye,
  bream, red fish and snapper,
  cut into large chunks
2 tablespoons chopped fresh flat-
  leaf parsley

Toasts
½ baguette, cut into twelve
  1.5 cm (5/8 inch) slices
2 large cloves garlic, halved

Rouille
3 slices day-old Italian white
  bread, crusts removed
1 red capsicum, seeded and
  quartered
1 small fresh red chilli, seeded
  and chopped
3 cloves garlic, crushed
1 tablespoon chopped fresh basil
  leaves
⅓ cup (80 ml/2¾ fl oz) olive oil

1 Heat the oil in a large saucepan over low heat. Cook the onion and leek for 5 minutes without browning. Add the garlic, chopped tomato and 1 tablespoon of the tomato paste. Simmer for 5 minutes. Stir in 2 litres cold water, then add parsley, bay leaves, thyme, fennel, saffron and seafood trimmings. Bring to the boil, then reduce the heat and simmer for 30–40 minutes.

2 Strain the stock into a large saucepan, pressing out the juices. Set aside ¼ cup (60 ml/2 fl oz) stock. Add the Pernod to the saucepan and stir in extra tomato paste if needed to enrich the colour. Season with salt and freshly ground black pepper. Bring to the boil and add the potato, then reduce the heat and simmer for 5 minutes.

3 Add the blue-eye and bream, cook for 2–3 minutes, then add the red fish and snapper, and cook for 5–6 minutes, or until cooked.

4 To make the toasts, toast the bread until golden on both sides. While still warm, rub with the garlic.

5 To make the rouille, soak the bread in enough cold water to cover, for 5 minutes. Cook the capsicum, skin-side up, under a hot grill until the skin blackens and blisters. Place in a plastic bag and leave to cool, then peel away the skin. Roughly chop the flesh. Squeeze the bread dry and place in a food processor with the capsicum, chilli, garlic and basil. Process to a smooth paste. With the motor running, gradually add the oil until the consistency resembles mayonnaise. Thin the sauce with 1–2 tablespoons of the reserved fish stock, and season to taste.

6 To serve, place 2 pieces of toast in the base of six soup bowls. Spoon in the soup and fish pieces and scatter some parsley over the top. Serve with the rouille.

NUTRITION PER SERVE
Protein 60 g; Fat 30 g; Carbohydrate 40 g; Dietary Fibre 5.5 g; Cholesterol 175 mg; 2838 kJ (678 cal)

NOTE: It is important to try to use at least four different varieties of fish, choosing a range of textures and flavours. Rascasse, where available, is traditional, but cod, bass, John dory, halibut, monkfish, turbot, hake and red mullet are also used. Shellfish such as lobster, scallops or mussels can be used.

Simmer the onion, leek, garlic, tomato and tomato paste for 5 minutes.

Cook the firmer-fleshed fish pieces slightly longer than the delicate pieces.

Rub the halved garlic cloves over the toasted bread slices.

Process the rouille until it is the consistency of mayonnaise.

FISH AND MACARONI CASSEROLE

Preparation time: 20 minutes
Total cooking time: 50 minutes
Serves 4

1 cup (155 g/5 oz) macaroni
30 g (1 oz) butter
1 onion, chopped
500 g (1 lb) white fish fillets, cut into 2 cm (¾ inch) cubes
1 tablespoon chopped fresh thyme
100 g (3½ oz) butter mushrooms, sliced
½ teaspoon hot English mustard
1 tablespoon plain flour
1 cup (250 ml/8 fl oz) chicken stock
½ cup (125 ml/4 fl oz) cream

½ cup (125 g/4 oz) sour cream
1 cup (80 g/2¾ oz) fresh breadcrumbs
1 cup (125 g/4 oz) grated Cheddar
½ cup (50 g/1¾ oz) grated fresh Parmesan
2 tablespoons chopped fresh parsley

1 Preheat the oven to moderate 180°C (350°F/Gas 4). Cook the macaroni in a large saucepan of rapidly boiling water until just tender. Drain and set aside.
2 Heat the butter in a heavy-based saucepan over medium heat. Cook the onion for 3 minutes, or until golden. Add the fish, thyme and mushrooms. Cook for 5 minutes, or until the fish is tender. Remove from the pan and keep warm.

3 Stir the mustard and flour into the pan. Add the stock and cream gradually. Stir constantly over medium heat for 3 minutes, or until the mixture boils and thickens. Boil for 1 minute, then remove from the heat. Stir in the sour cream.
4 Transfer the mixture to a large bowl, and stir in the macaroni, fish and mushrooms. Spoon into a large ovenproof dish. Combine the breadcrumbs, cheese and parsley. Sprinkle over the macaroni mixture. Bake for 30 minutes, or until golden. Serve with a green salad.

NUTRITION PER SERVE
Protein 49 g; Fat 50 g; Carbohydrate 46 g; Dietary Fibre 3.5 g; Cholesterol 217 mg; 3465 kJ (830 cal)

Cook the macaroni in a large saucepan of boiling water until just tender.

Add the fish, thyme and mushrooms to the pan, and cook until the fish is tender.

Gradually add the stock and cream, stirring until the mixture boils and thickens.

CREAMY FISH CASSEROLE

Preparation time: 10 minutes
Total cooking time: 1 hour
Serves 4

2 large potatoes, chopped
¼ cup (60 ml/2 fl oz) milk or
 cream
1 egg
60 g (2 oz) butter
½ cup (60 g/2 oz) grated Cheddar
800 g (1 lb 10 oz) white fish
 fillets, cut into large chunks
1½ cups (375 ml/12 fl oz) milk,
 extra
1 onion, finely chopped
1 clove garlic, crushed
2 tablespoons plain flour

2 tablespoons lemon juice
2 teaspoons lemon rind
1 tablespoon chopped fresh dill

1 Preheat the oven to moderate 180°C (350°F/Gas 4). Boil or steam the potato for 8 minutes, or until tender. Drain and mash with the milk or cream, egg and half the butter. Mix in half the cheese, then set aside.
2 Put the fish in a shallow frying pan and cover with the extra milk. Bring to the boil, then reduce the heat and simmer for 2–3 minutes, or until the fish flakes easily. Drain the fish well, reserving the milk, and put in a 1.5 litre ovenproof dish.
3 Melt the remaining butter over medium heat in a saucepan and cook the onion and garlic for 2 minutes.

Stir in the flour and cook for 1 minute, or until golden. Remove from the heat and gradually stir in the reserved milk. Return to the heat and stir constantly until the sauce boils and thickens. Reduce the heat and simmer for 2 minutes. Add the lemon juice, rind and dill, and season. Mix with the fish, cover with potato and sprinkle with the remaining cheese. Bake for 35 minutes, or until golden.

NUTRITION PER SERVE
Protein 54 g; Fat 29 g; Carbohydrate 24 g; Dietary Fibre 2.5 g; Cholesterol 253 mg; 2390 kJ (570 cal)

NOTE: You could use ling, perch, hake or snapper.

Cook the fish in the simmering milk until it flakes easily when tested.

Stir the flour into the onion and garlic, and cook until golden.

Using two spoons, cover the fish mixture with the mashed potato.

SOBA NOODLE AND VEGETABLE SOUP

Preparation time: 15 minutes +
  5 minutes soaking
Total cooking time: 10 minutes
Serves 4

250 g (8 oz) soba noodles
2 dried shiitake mushrooms
2 litres vegetable stock
120 g (4 oz) snow peas, cut into
  thin strips
2 small carrots, cut into thin 5
  cm (2 inch) strips
2 cloves garlic, finely chopped

6 spring onions, cut into 5 cm
  (2 inch) lengths and thinly
  sliced lengthways
3 cm (1¼ inch) piece fresh
  ginger, julienned
⅓ cup (80 ml/2¾ fl oz) soy sauce
¼ cup (60 ml/2 fl oz) mirin or
  sake
1 cup (90 g/3 oz) bean sprouts

1 Cook the noodles according to the packet instructions, then drain.
2 Soak the mushrooms in ½ cup (125 ml/4 fl oz) boiling water until soft. Drain, reserving the liquid. Discard the stems and slice the caps.
3 Combine the vegetable stock, mushrooms, reserved liquid, snow peas, carrot, garlic, spring onion and ginger in a large saucepan. Bring slowly to the boil, then reduce the heat to low and simmer for 5 minutes, or until the vegetables are tender. Add the soy sauce, mirin and bean sprouts. Cook for a further 3 minutes.
4 Divide the noodles among four large serving bowls. Ladle the hot liquid and vegetables over the top and garnish with coriander.

NUTRITION PER SERVE
Protein 13 g; Fat 1.5 g; Carbohydrate 30 g;
Dietary Fibre 6 g; Cholesterol 11 mg;
1124 kJ (270 cal)

Cut the ginger into julienne strips (thin strips the size and shape of matchsticks).

After soaking the mushrooms, drain and thinly slice them.

Simmer the vegetables for 5 minutes, or until they are tender.

VEGETARIAN CHILLI

Preparation time: 15 minutes + 10
minutes soaking
Total cooking time: 40 minutes
Serves 6–8

¾ cup (130 g/4½ oz) burghul
  (cracked wheat)
2 tablespoons olive oil
1 large onion, finely chopped
2 cloves garlic, crushed
1 teaspoon chilli powder
2 teaspoons ground cumin
1 teaspoon cayenne pepper
½ teaspoon ground cinnamon

2 x 400 g (13 oz) cans crushed
  tomatoes
3 cups (750 ml/24 fl oz) vegetable
  stock
440 g (14 oz) can red kidney
  beans, rinsed and drained
2 x 300 g (10 oz) cans chickpeas,
  rinsed and drained
310 g (10 oz) can corn kernels,
  drained
2 tablespoons tomato paste
corn chips and sour cream

1 Soak the burghul with 1 cup (250
ml/8 fl oz) hot water for 10 minutes.
Heat the oil in a large heavy-based
saucepan and cook the onion for 10
minutes, stirring often, until soft and
golden.
2 Add the garlic, chilli powder,
cumin, cayenne and cinnamon, and
cook, stirring, for 1 minute.
3 Add the tomato, stock and burghul.
Bring to the boil and simmer for 10
minutes. Stir in the beans, drained
chickpeas, corn and tomato paste,
and simmer for 20 minutes, stirring
often. Serve with corn chips and
sour cream.

NUTRITION PER SERVE (8)
Protein 7 g; Fat 10 g; Carbohydrate 18 g;
Dietary Fibre 7 g; Cholesterol 8 mg; 780
kJ (185 cal)

*Stir the garlic and spices into the pan with
the onion, and cook for 1 minute.*

*Add the crushed tomato, stock and
burghul to the pan.*

*Stir in the beans, chickpeas, corn kernels
and tomato paste.*

VEGETABLE STEW WITH COUSCOUS

Preparation time: 30 minutes
Total cooking time: 45 minutes
Serves 4

2 tablespoons olive oil
1 onion, sliced
2 teaspoons yellow mustard
   seeds
2 teaspoons ground cumin
1 teaspoon paprika
1 clove garlic, crushed
2 teaspoons grated fresh ginger
2 sticks celery, chopped
2 carrots, peeled and chopped
2 small parsnips, peeled and cubed

300 g (10 oz) pumpkin, diced
2 zucchini, halved and thickly
   sliced
1½ cups (375 ml/12 fl oz)
   vegetable stock
1 cup (185 g/6 oz) instant
   couscous
30 g (1 oz) butter, diced
harissa, to taste

1 Heat the oil in a large, heavy-based pan. Add the onion and cook over medium heat for 10 minutes, or until very soft and lightly golden, stirring occasionally.
2 Add the mustard seeds, cumin, paprika, garlic and ginger and stir for 1 minute. Add all the vegetables and stir to coat. Add the stock, bring to

the boil, then reduce the heat and simmer, partially covered, for about 30 minutes, or until tender.
3 Place the couscous in a heatproof bowl. Add ¾ cup (185 ml/6 fl oz) of boiling water and leave to stand for 2 minutes. Add the butter, then fluff up the grains with a fork, stirring through the butter. Serve with the vegetables and a little harissa.

NUTRITION PER SERVE
Protein 7 g; Fat 17 g; Carbohydrate 40 g; Dietary Fibre 5 g; Cholesterol 20 mg; 1345 kJ (320 cal)

COOK'S FILE

Note: Harissa is a fiery relish made of ground chillies and spices. You will find it in speciality stores.

Chop the celery and peeled carrots into evenly sized pieces.

Fry the onions in the oil over medium heat until soft and golden.

Add the butter to the couscous and fluff up the grains using a fork.

CHILLI BEANS

Preparation time: 45 minutes +
  overnight soaking
Total cooking time: 1 hour 35 minutes
Serves 4–6

½ cup (110 g/3½ oz) dried black
  beans
½ cup (110 g/3½ oz) dried pinto
  beans
½ cup (110 g/3½ oz) dried
  chickpeas
2 small red chillies
1 small green chilli
1 tablespoon olive oil
1 onion, sliced
4 cloves garlic, finely chopped
4 cm (1½ inch) piece fresh
  ginger, finely chopped
¼ teaspoon chilli powder
2 teaspoons ground cumin
2 teaspoons ground coriander
1 litre vegetable stock
440 g (14 oz) can chopped
  tomatoes
1 small red capsicum, diced
1 small yellow capsicum, diced
¼ cup (7 g/¼ oz) chopped
  coriander leaves
¼ cup (60 ml/2 fl oz) lime juice

1 Cover the beans and chickpeas in boiling water and soak overnight. Drain and rinse well.
2 Discard the seeds and membranes from chillies. Chop finely; set aside.
3 Heat the oil in a large pan. Cook the onion over low heat for 5 minutes, or until soft and transparent. Add the garlic, ginger, chillies, ground spices, stock, beans and chickpeas. Bring to the boil, reduce the heat, cover and simmer for 1 hour. (There should be just enough liquid to coat the beans.)
4 Add the tomatoes and the red and yellow capsicums and simmer gently for 30 minutes, or until the capsicum and beans are tender. Stir in the coriander leaves and lime juice. Season to taste with salt and freshly cracked pepper and serve.

NUTRITION PER SERVE (6)
Protein 10 g; Fat 5 g; Carbohydrate 20 g; Dietary Fibre 9 g; Cholesterol 0 mg; 711 kJ (170 cal)

Cover the dried beans and chickpeas with boiling water and leave to soak overnight.

Remove the seeds and membranes from the red and green chillies.

Add the drained beans and chickpeas to the spiced stock mixture.

TOMATO AND POTATO STEW

Preparation time: 30 minutes
Total cooking time: 1 hour 15 minutes
Serves 6

¼ cup (60 ml/2 fl oz) olive oil
2 red capsicums, chopped
2 green capsicums, chopped
3 onions, thinly sliced
4 cloves garlic, crushed
2 x 400 g (13 oz) cans chopped
   tomatoes
3–4 sprigs of thyme, and extra to
   garnish
2 bay leaves
2 teaspoons caster sugar
1.2 kg (2 lb 7 oz) potatoes, cut
   into chunks
1 cup (125 g/4 oz) black olives,
   pitted
small block of Parmesan, for
   shaving

1 Heat the oil in a large, heavy-based pan. When the oil is hot, cook the capsicum, onion and garlic over medium heat for 10 minutes, or until softened. Add the chopped tomatoes, ½ cup (125 ml/4 fl oz) water, thyme sprigs, bay leaves and sugar. Season to taste and leave to simmer gently for 15 minutes.
2 Add the potato chunks, cover and cook very gently for 50–60 minutes, or until tender. Stir in the olives.
3 Using a vegetable peeler, carefully shave thin slivers from the Parmesan block, arrange over the stew and garnish with a sprig of thyme.

NUTRITION PER SERVE
Protein 10 g; Fat 12 g; Carbohydrate 40 g; Dietary Fibre 9 g; Cholesterol 3 mg; 1330 kJ (320 cal)

When the oil in the pan is hot, fry the capsicum, onion and garlic until soft.

Add the potato chunks to the tomato sauce mixture.

Using a vegetable peeler, carefully shave thin slivers from the Parmesan block.

LENTIL BHUJIA STEW

Preparation time: 30 minutes +
  overnight soaking + 30 minutes
  refrigeration
Total cooking time: 1 hour 10 minutes
Serves 4–6

2 cups (370 g/12 oz) green or
  brown lentils
1 large onion, grated
1 large potato, grated
1 teaspoon ground cumin
1 teaspoon ground coriander
1 teaspoon ground turmeric
¾ cup (90 g/3 oz) plain flour
oil, for shallow-frying
2 cloves garlic, crushed
1 tablespoon grated fresh ginger
1 cup (250 ml/8 fl oz) tomato
  purée
2 cups (500 ml/16 fl oz) vegetable
  stock
1 cup (250 ml/8 fl oz) cream
200 g (6½ oz) green beans,
  topped, tailed and cut in half
2 carrots, sliced
2 hard-boiled eggs, chopped
sprig of rosemary, to garnish

1 Soak the lentils overnight in cold water. Drain well. Squeeze the excess moisture from the lentils, onion and potato using a tea towel. Place them in a bowl with the ground spices and flour; mix well and leave for 10 minutes. With floured hands, shape the mixture into walnut-sized balls and place on a foil-lined tray. Cover and refrigerate for 30 minutes.
2 Heat 2 cm (¾ inch) of oil in a heavy-based pan. Cook the balls in batches over high heat until golden brown. Drain on paper towels.
3 Heat 2 tablespoons of oil in a pan; gently fry the garlic and ginger for 2 minutes. Stir in the purée, stock and cream. Bring to the boil, reduce the heat and simmer for 10 minutes. Add the beans, lentil balls and carrots. Cook, covered, for 30 minutes, stirring twice. Add the egg; cook for 10 minutes. Garnish with rosemary to serve.

NUTRITION PER SERVE (6)
Protein 23 g; Fat 30 g; Carbohydrate 45 g; Dietary Fibre 13 g; Cholesterol 125 mg; 2290 kJ (550 cal)

COOK'S FILE

Variation: Split peas can be used in this recipe in place of the lentils. Soak them in cold water overnight, then drain well before using.

Shape the lentil mixture into walnut-sized balls. Place on a foil-lined tray.

Fry the lentil balls in oil in batches over high heat, until golden brown.

Add the beans, lentil balls and carrots to the simmering sauce.

CASSEROLE OF AUTUMN VEGETABLES

Preparation time: 25 minutes
Total cooking time: 30 minutes
Serves 4–6

185 g (6 oz) frozen broad beans, thawed
150 g (5 oz) pickling onions
50 g (1¾ oz) butter
2 teaspoons olive oil
400 g (13 oz) small parsnips
150 g (5 oz) Jerusalem artichokes
2 tablespoons plain flour
2⅓ cups (600 ml/20 fl oz) chicken stock
300 ml (10 fl oz) cream
2 teaspoons grated lemon rind
1 teaspoon grated orange rind
400 g (13 oz) baby carrots, trimmed
500 g (1 lb) baby turnips, trimmed

1 Peel and discard the tough outer skin of the broad beans. Carefully peel the onions, leaving the flat root end attached, then cut a cross through the root end of each onion.
2 Heat the butter and oil in a large, heavy-based pan until foamy. Add the onions and cook for 7 minutes over low-medium heat, turning often to colour evenly.
3 While the onions are browning, peel the parsnips and artichokes and cut into bite-sized pieces. Add to the pan and toss well. Scatter with the flour, toss to coat and cook for 2 minutes.
4 Stir in the stock, cream and rinds. Bring to the boil, stirring, then reduce the heat and simmer for 7 minutes, or until the vegetables are half-cooked.
5 Add the carrots and turnips; toss well. Cover and cook for 4–5 minutes, or until the vegetables are just tender. Season well with salt and freshly ground pepper, stir in the broad beans to heat through, and serve.

NUTRITION PER SERVE (6)
Protein 7 g; Fat 30 g; Carbohydrate 25 g; Dietary Fibre 10 g; Cholesterol 90 mg; 1665 kJ (400 cal)

COOK'S FILE

NOTES: Baby vegetables have a sweet, delicate flavour. If unavailable, choose the smallest vegetables and cook them for a few minutes longer.

Skin the broad beans and cut a cross through the root end of the peeled onions.

Peel the small parsnips and Jerusalem artichokes and cut into bite-sized pieces.

CHICKPEA AND HERB DUMPLING SOUP

Preparation time: 30 minutes
Total cooking time: 35 minutes
Serves 4

1 tablespoon oil
1 onion, chopped
2 cloves garlic, crushed
2 teaspoons ground cumin
1 teaspoon ground coriander
¼ teaspoon chilli powder
2 x 300 g (10 oz) cans chickpeas, drained
3½ cups (875 ml/28 fl oz) vegetable stock
2 x 425 g (14 oz) cans chopped tomatoes
1 tablespoon chopped fresh coriander leaves
1 cup (125 g/4 oz) self-raising flour
25 g (¾ oz) butter, chopped
2 tablespoons grated fresh Parmesan
2 tablespoons mixed chopped fresh herbs (chives, flat-leaf parsley and coriander leaves)
¼ cup (60 ml/2 fl oz) milk

1 Heat the oil in a large saucepan and cook the onion over medium heat for 2–3 minutes, or until soft. Add the garlic, cumin, ground coriander and chilli, and cook for 1 minute, or until fragrant. Add the chickpeas, stock and tomato. Bring to the boil, then reduce the heat and simmer, covered, for 10 minutes. Stir in the coriander.

2 To make the dumplings, sift the flour into a bowl and add the chopped butter. Rub the butter into the flour with your fingertips until it resembles fine breadcrumbs. Stir in the cheese and mixed fresh herbs. Make a well in the centre, add the milk and mix with a flat-bladed knife until just combined. Bring the dough together into a rough ball, divide into eight portions and roll into small balls.

3 Add the dumplings to the soup, cover and simmer for 20 minutes, or until a skewer comes out clean when inserted into the centre of the dumplings.

NUTRITION PER SERVE
Protein 17 g; Fat 16 g; Carbohydrate 50 g; Dietary Fibre 12 g; Cholesterol 23 mg; 1767 kJ (422 cal)

Stir the chopped coriander into the simmering chickpea mixture.

Add the milk to the dumpling mixture and mix with a flat-bladed knife.

Pierce the dumplings with a skewer to test if they are cooked.

CHANNA MASALA (CHICKPEA CURRY)

Preparation time: 10 minutes +
    overnight soaking
Total cooking time: 1 hour 15 minutes
Serves 6

1 cup (220 g/7 oz) dried
    chickpeas
2 tablespoons oil
2 onions, finely chopped
2 large ripe tomatoes, chopped
½ teaspoon ground coriander
1 teaspoon ground cumin
1 teaspoon chilli powder
¼ teaspoon ground turmeric
1 tablespoon channa (chole)
    masala
20 g (¾ oz) ghee or butter
1 small white onion, sliced
fresh mint and coriander leaves,
    to garnish

1 Place the chickpeas in a bowl, cover with water and leave to soak overnight. Drain, rinse and place in a large saucepan. Cover with plenty of water and bring to the boil, then reduce the heat and simmer for 40 minutes, or until soft. Drain.

2 Heat the oil in a large saucepan, add the onion and cook over medium heat for 15 minutes, or until golden brown. Add the tomato, ground coriander and cumin, chilli powder, turmeric, channa (chole) masala and 2 cups (500 ml/16 fl oz) cold water, and cook for 10 minutes, or until the tomato is soft. Add the chickpeas, season well with salt and cook for 7–10 minutes, or until the sauce thickens. Transfer to a serving dish. Place the ghee or butter on top and allow to melt before serving. Garnish with sliced onion and fresh mint and coriander leaves.

NUTRITION PER SERVE
Protein 8 g; Fat 11 g; Carbohydrate 17 g; Dietary Fibre 6 g; Cholesterol 8.5 mg; 835 kJ (200 cal)

NOTE: Channa (chole) masala is a spice blend specifically used in this dish. It is available at Indian grocery stores. Garam masala can be used as a substitute, but this will alter the final flavour.

Cook the onion in a large saucepan until it is golden brown.

Add the drained chickpeas and cook until the sauce has thickened.

POLENTA WITH SPICY VEGETABLES

Preparation time: 30 minutes
Total cooking time: 1 hour 10 minutes
Serves 4

1 tablespoon olive oil
1 large onion, sliced
4 cloves garlic, finely chopped
¼ teaspoon chilli powder
2 teaspoons ground cumin
2 teaspoons ground coriander
½ teaspoon ground turmeric
½ teaspoon ground cinnamon
2 potatoes, cubed
3 carrots, thickly sliced
1½ cups (375 ml/12 fl oz)
    vegetable stock
300 g (10 oz) baby yellow squash,
    halved
3 zucchini, cut into chunks
300 g (10 oz) pumpkin, cut into
    chunks
2 tablespoons chopped parsley

Polenta
1 litre vegetable stock or water
1⅔ cups (250 g/8 oz) fine polenta
100 g (3½ oz) butter, chopped
⅓ cup (35 g/1¼ oz) finely grated
    fresh Parmesan

1 Heat the oil in a large saucepan. Fry the onion over low heat for 5 minutes, or until soft and translucent. Add the garlic and spices and cook over medium heat for 3 minutes.
2 Add the potato, carrot and stock. Bring to the boil, reduce the heat, then cover and simmer for 10 minutes.
3 Add the squash and zucchini. Cover partially and simmer for 15 minutes. Add the pumpkin; cook for 10 minutes more, or until the vegetables are soft and the mixture is thick and gravy-like. Season well with salt and freshly cracked pepper. Remove from the heat, cover and keep warm.
4 To make the polenta, bring the stock to the boil. Add the polenta in a thin stream, stirring constantly with a wooden spoon. Simmer gently for 20 minutes, stirring constantly so it doesn't stick. When thick, add the butter and Parmesan and mix until melted. Season well and serve at once.
5 Stir the parsley into the vegetables. Spoon the polenta onto serving plates, swirling it into nests with a hole in the centre. Spoon in the spicy vegetables and serve immediately.

NUTRITION PER SERVE
Protein 15 g; Fat 30 g; Carbohydrate 65 g; Dietary Fibre 9.5 g; Cholesterol 72 mg; 2485 kJ (595 cal)

Add the pumpkin to the partially cooked vegetable mixture.

Simmer the polenta gently for 20 minutes, stirring constantly until thick.

When the polenta has thickened, add the butter and Parmesan. Stir until melted.

CASSEROLE OF CURRIED VEGETABLES

Preparation time: 25 minutes
Total cooking time: 1 hour 25 minutes
Serves 4–6

1 tablespoon vegetable oil
1 leek, thickly sliced
2–3 cloves garlic, crushed
1 stick celery, thickly sliced
1 large carrot
1 large parsnip
1 large potato
1 medium swede or turnip
500 g (1 lb) sweet potato
500 g (1 lb) pumpkin
280 g (9 oz) can curried cooking
    sauce
400 ml (13 fl oz) coconut milk
1 cup (155 g/5 oz) shelled fresh
    green peas
½ cup (15 g/½ oz) chopped
    coriander leaves

1 Preheat the oven to moderate 180°C (350°F/Gas 4). Heat the oil in a large flameproof casserole dish. Cook the leek, garlic and celery over medium heat for 2–3 minutes, or until tender. Remove the pan from the heat.
2 Peel the root vegetables and cut into 5 cm (2 inch) pieces. Add them to the dish, place over medium heat and stir well to combine. Stir in the curry sauce and coconut milk and cook, stirring, for 2–3 minutes.
3 Cover and bake for about 1¼ hours, or until the vegetables are tender, stirring gently once or twice.
4 Meanwhile, cook the peas in boiling water until just tender. Drain, refresh under cold water and stir into the casserole with the coriander leaves. Serve immediately.

NUTRITION PER SERVE (6)
Protein 8 g; Fat 25 g; Carbohydrate 35 g; Dietary Fibre 9 g; Cholesterol 4 mg; 1540 kJ (370 cal)

COOK'S FILE

Notes: Curried cooking sauces are not to be confused with concentrated curry pastes. They are available in many brands and flavours, ranging from mild to hot. Choose one to suit your taste.
• If fresh peas are not available, frozen peas can be substituted.

In a flameproof casserole dish, fry the leek, garlic and celery until tender.

Peel the root vegetables and cut them into 5 cm (2 inch) pieces.

VEGETABLE TAGINE

Preparation time: 20 minutes
Total cooking time: 1 hour
Serves 4–6

2 tablespoons oil
2 onions, chopped
1 teaspoon ground ginger
2 teaspoons ground paprika
2 teaspoons ground cumin
1 cinnamon stick
pinch saffron threads
1.5 kg (3 lb) vegetables, peeled and cut into large chunks (carrot, eggplant, orange sweet potato, parsnip, potato, pumpkin)
½ preserved lemon, rinsed, pith and flesh removed, thinly sliced
400 g (13 oz) can peeled tomatoes
1 cup (250 ml/8 fl oz) vegetable stock
100 g (3½ oz) dried pears, halved
50 g (1¾ oz) pitted prunes
2 zucchini, cut into large chunks
300 g (10 oz) couscous
1 tablespoon olive oil
¼ cup (7 g/¼ oz) chopped fresh flat-leaf parsley
⅓ cup (50 g/1¾ oz) almonds

1 Preheat the oven to moderate 180°C (350°F/Gas 4). Heat the oil in a large saucepan or ovenproof dish, add the onion and cook over medium heat for 5 minutes, or until soft. Add the spices and cook for 3 minutes.
2 Add the vegetables and cook, stirring, until coated with the spices and the vegetables begin to soften. Add the lemon, tomatoes, stock, pears and prunes. Cover, transfer to the oven and cook for 30 minutes.

Add the zucchini and cook for 15–20 minutes, or until the vegetables are tender.
3 Cover the couscous with the olive oil and 2 cups (500 ml/16 fl oz) boiling water, and stand until all the water has been absorbed. Fluff with a fork.
4 Remove the cinnamon stick from

the vegetables, then stir in the parsley. Serve on a large platter with the couscous formed into a ring and the vegetable tagine in the centre, sprinkled with the almonds.

NUTRITION PER SERVE (6)
Protein 8 g; Fat 15 g; Carbohydrate 33 g; Dietary Fibre 9 g; Cholesterol 0 mg; 1240 kJ (296 cal)

Cook the vegetables until they are coated in the spices and start to soften.

Once all the water has been absorbed, fluff the couscous with a fork.

Before serving, remove the cinnamon stick from the tagine.

SPICY VEGETABLE STEW WITH DHAL

Preparation time: 25 minutes +
  2 hours soaking
Total cooking time: 1 hour 35 minutes
Serves 4–6

DHAL
¾ cup (165 g/5½ oz) yellow split
  peas
5 cm (2 inch) piece fresh ginger,
  grated
2–3 cloves garlic, crushed
1 fresh red chilli, seeded and
  chopped

2 tablespoons oil
1 teaspoon yellow mustard seeds
1 teaspoon cumin seeds
1 teaspoon ground cumin
½ teaspoon garam masala
1 red onion, cut into thin wedges
3 tomatoes, peeled, seeded and
  chopped
3 slender eggplants, cut into
  2 cm (¾ inch) slices
2 carrots, cut into 2 cm (¾ inch)
  slices
¼ cauliflower, cut into florets
1½ cups (375 ml/12 fl oz)
  vegetable stock
2 small zucchini, cut into 3 cm
  (1¼ inch) slices
½ cup (80 g/2¾ oz) frozen peas
½ cup (15 g/½ oz) fresh
  coriander leaves

1 To make the dhal, place the split peas in a bowl, cover with water and soak for 2 hours. Drain. Place in a large saucepan with the ginger, garlic, chilli and 3 cups (750 ml/24 fl oz) water. Bring to the boil, then reduce the heat and simmer for 45 minutes, or until soft.

2 Heat the oil in a large saucepan. Cook the spices over medium heat for 30 seconds, or until fragrant. Add the onion and cook for a further 2 minutes, or until the onion is soft. Stir in the tomato, eggplant, carrot and cauliflower.

3 Add the dhal purée and stock, mix together well and simmer, covered, for 45 minutes, or until the vegetables are tender. Stir occasionally. Add the zucchini and peas during the last 10 minutes of cooking. Stir in the coriander leaves and serve hot.

NUTRITION PER SERVE (6)
Protein 11 g; Fat 7 g; Carbohydrate 20 g; Dietary Fibre 8.5 g; Cholesterol 17 mg; 780 kJ (186 cal)

Peel the skin from the tomatoes, then remove the seeds and chop.

Simmer the dhal mixture for 45 minutes, or until the split peas are soft.

Simmer, covered, until the vegetables are tender, stirring occasionally.

INDEX

First Published 2004 by Murdoch Books, Pty Limited.

Erico House, 6th Floor North, 93-99 Upper Richmond Road, Putney London SW15 2TG.

This wiro-bound edition published 2006 for INDEX: Henson Way, Kettering, NN16 8PX, United Kingdom

Chief Executive: Juliet Rogers
Publisher: Kay Scarlett.

ISBN 1 74045 848 6   A catalogue record of this book is available from the British Library.
Printed in China by 1010 Printing International Limited.

The nutritional information provided for each recipe does not include any accompaniments, such as rice, unless they are listed in the ingredients. The values are approximations and can be affected by biological and seasonal variations in food, the unknown composition of some manufactured foods and uncertainty in the dietary database. Nutrient data given are derived primarily from the NUTTAB95 database produced by the Australian New Zealand Food Authority.